Endor

"*Becoming Whole* is a book and training manual offering mental health professionals, pastors and laymen a comprehensive and step-by-step process of partnering with God through Wholeness Prayer to apply His truth and His presence in the healing of life's wounds. Combining principles from the disciplines of psychology, cognitive-behavioral therapy, personality theory and Biblical truths, Jean Coles has authored an in-depth practical and encouraging resource for those involved in the healing of persons. I believe it works best as a training manual for those wishing to learn more about how to apply the power of God through healing prayer, as well as for those who are willing to dig in, explore and learn from the book and additional resources offered by the author. This book offers refreshing and powerful tools that can change people's lives."
   ~ **Dr. David Wickstrom**, Ph.D., Clinical Psychologist

"*Becoming Whole: The Power of Wholeness Prayer* invites us into the heart of Jean Coles' work over the past sixteen years, a prayer focus which has proven effective in helping many people. *Becoming Whole* offers weary souls a very personal, practical and delightful pathway through the woods: resting by cool springs, pouring the refreshing water of deep prayer upon pain, fear, loss and more – inviting Jesus to speak and heal."
   ~ **John Splinter**, M.C.E., M.A., Ph.D.
      Director of Member Health, *Beyond* (beyond.org)

"*Becoming Whole* fully meets my criteria for an outstanding book. No other book, to my knowledge, so clearly outlines a pattern for prayer that so effectively addresses and brings healing to such a broad area of emotional, mental, relational, and spiritual dysfunction. This prayer pattern—called "The 5 R's of Wholeness Prayer"—is constructed on and supported by Biblical principles. Jean explains the 5 R steps in a way that is easy to understand and to follow. Over time and in numerous settings, Wholeness Prayer has proven to be an effective strategy in connecting the healing power of the Holy Spirit with the present and past wounds of Christian believers. It works with anyone who is willing to open their heart to Jesus. With confidence, I recommend *Becoming*

Whole as an invaluable resource for every Christian counselor and teacher, as well as other prayer warriors."
~ **Jane Ault**, Counselor, Author of *Emotional Freedom*

"For decades Jean Coles has been a student of the way God comes to the broken and bound and leads them into wholeness and freedom in Jesus. *Becoming Whole* gathers up her years of learning and lays out a comprehensive course on the practice and principles of Wholeness Prayer. Wholeness Prayer holds out hope to the hopeless. Many, through this way of prayer, have finally been able to take hold of the hope of the gospel and be hauled up out of the pit of their despair to solid, high ground in Christ. If you long for this kind of rescue or know someone who does, hope is here."
~ **Mark Beazley**
Wholeness Prayer Trainer and Practitioner

"AWESOME BOOK! *Becoming Whole* is full-blown amazing. Reading this book by Jean Coles was a magnificent experience. I enjoyed learning about Wholeness Prayer in a systematic order that was very follow-able and easy to understand. I see people referencing *Becoming Whole* many times after they have already read through it once, to refresh and review; there is so much good material in this book. The testimonies are very powerful and inspire me to keep on reading and go further in my own victories."
~ **Catherine Dicus**, Recipient of Wholeness Prayer

Becoming Whole

The Power of Wholeness Prayer

Jean Coles

Becoming Whole: The Power of Wholeness Prayer

© 2017 Jean Coles, Freedom for the Captives Ministries
www.freemin.org

Permission is granted to copy these materials for non-commercial use, provided that copyright and source statements remain intact, and the Bible verses copied account for
less than 25 percent of the total portion of the copied text.

Scripture quotations marked NIV are taken from the Holy Bible, New International Version®, NIV®. Copyright © 1973, 1978, 1984, 2011 by Biblica, Inc.™ Used by permission of Zondervan. All rights reserved worldwide. www.zondervan.com The "NIV" and "New International Version" are trademarks registered in the United States Patent and Trademark Office by Biblica, Inc.™

Scripture quotations marked NASB are from the New American Standard Bible®, Copyright © 1960, 1962, 1963, 1968, 1971, 1972, 1973, 1975, 1977, 1995 by The Lockman Foundation.
Used by permission. (www.Lockman.org).

Scripture quotations marked ESV are from the ESV® Bible (The Holy Bible, English Standard Version®), copyright © 2001 by Crossway, a publishing ministry of Good News Publishers.
Used by permission. All rights reserved.

Testimonies included in this book are anonymous and have been edited for clarity. Examples of Wholeness Prayer times are representative experiences of actual people who have gained increased freedom through Wholeness Prayer. Identifying details have been changed to protect confidentiality.

Cover Photo: "United by God" quilted Bali batik wall hanging, inspired by Picasso's "The Dance of Youth."

This ebook and other resources are available at www.freemin.org.

Our Father who is in heaven,
Hallowed be Your name.
Your kingdom come.
Your will be done,
On earth as it is in heaven.

~Matthew 6:9b-10 (NASB)

Contents

Foreword by John Ault   xiii

Preface   xv

Introduction   xix
    Tips for Using this Book   xxi

Part 1. Basic Wholeness Prayer   1
    Chapter 1. Finding Freedom   3
    Chapter 2. The Basic Framework of Wholeness Prayer   7
        1. How Can We "Get Our Stuff Back"?   8
        2. The Wholeness Prayer Framework   8
        3. Diagram of the Wholeness Prayer Process   13
    Chapter 3. Representative Scenarios   15
        1. Scenario 1: Sam and Mike   15
        2. Scenario 2: Diane and Marie   22
    Chapter 4. Basic Principles and Guidelines   33
    Chapter 5. Hindrances to Wholeness Prayer   43

Part 2. Keys for Nine Common Issues   51
    Chapter 6. Freedom from Generational Bondage   53
    Chapter 7. Freedom from Occult Bondage   59
    Chapter 8. Healing from Emotional Wounds   67
        1. Emotional Wounds Based on False Beliefs   69
        2. Unpleasant Emotions Based on Truth   71
        3. Anger   72
    Chapter 9. Replacing Curses with Blessings   75
    Chapter 10. Understanding God's Character   79
    Chapter 11. Praying Through Trauma   83
        1. Truth Revealed in a Traumatic Sequence of Events   88
        2. Applications to Abuse   89
    Chapter 12. Grieving Life's Losses   93
    Chapter 13. Confessing and Turning from Sin   99
    Chapter 14. Forgiving Others   101

Part 3. Keys for Additional Situations — 105

    Chapter 15. Forgiving One's Parents — 107
    Chapter 16. Forgiving and Accepting Oneself — 113
        1. Forgiving Oneself — 113
        2. Accepting Oneself — 116
    Chapter 17. Developing Healthy Boundaries — 119
    Chapter 18. Breaking Unholy Covenants — 123
    Chapter 19. Breaking Unholy One-Flesh Bonds — 127
    Chapter 20. Breaking Internal Strongholds — 129
        1. Unwise Decisions — 131
        2. Unhealthy Vows — 132
        3. Negative Scripts — 133
        4. Cursing Others — 134
        5. Feeling Cursed — 135
        6. Feeling Judged — 138
        7. Judging Others — 139
        8. Unhealthy Emotional Bonds — 140
    Chapter 21. Replacing Counterfeit Desires — 143
    Chapter 22. Overcoming Unhealthy Fear — 145
        1. Replacing Fear Bonds with Love Bonds — 147
        2. Applications for Panic Attacks — 149
        3. No Longer a Victim – Empowered by a Loving God — 151
    Chapter 23. Finding True Security — 155
    Chapter 24. Developing Healthy Patterns — 159
        1. Example — 163
        2. Pattern for Overcoming Anxiety — 165
        3. Escaping a Looping Bowtie Pattern — 166
        4. Freedom from the Drama Triangle — 168
        5. Applications for Obsessive-Compulsive Behavior — 170
    Chapter 25. Giving Up Unhealthy Control — 171
    Chapter 26. Overcoming Perfectionism — 175
    Chapter 27. Overcoming Addictions — 179
        1. Overcoming Addiction to Pornography — 184
        2. Diagram of Addictive Behavior — 184
        3. Keys for Overcoming Addictions — 186
        4. Applications for Eating Disorders — 186
    Chapter 28. Addressing Unhealthy Relationship Styles — 189

Part 4. Applications to a Variety of Contexts — 195
Chapter 29. The 5 R's in Multiple Spheres — 197
Chapter 30. Applications for Physical Healing — 201
Chapter 31. Applications for Evangelism — 205
Chapter 32. Applications for Discipleship — 207
Chapter 33. Applications for Conflict Resolution — 213
  1. React or Respond? — 214
  2. Factors Involved in Conflict — 215
  3. Foundational Principles for Addressing Conflict — 216
  4. Helping Others Navigate Conflict Well — 218
  5. Applications for Married Couples — 220
  6. Resources — 221
Chapter 34. Applications for Spiritual Warfare — 223
  1. Addressing Spiritual Oppression — 224
  2. The Weapons of Our Warfare — 225

Epilogue. Where Will You Go from Here? — 227
1. Questions for Reflection — 227
2. My Prayer — 227

Appendices — 229
Appendix 1. Facilitating a Time of Wholeness Prayer — 229
Appendix 2. Other Freedom for the Captives Resources — 233
Appendix 3. Keys Used in Wholeness Prayer — 235
Appendix 4. Biblical Foundations of Wholeness — 243

Endnotes — 247

Foreword

Scripture lists being "renewed in the spirit of our mind" (Ephesians 4:23) as a key step in the transformation of our lifestyles. *Becoming Whole: The Power of Wholeness Prayer* gives very practical steps on how to appropriate this renewal in our minds.

Paul prayed for the Ephesians (1:17-19) to have an experiential revelation of knowledge about who they are in Christ. This sets forth the principle that prayer is an essential ingredient for a transformed mind. In *Becoming Whole*, Jean Coles leads readers through helpful prayer steps so they can experience those revelation experiences – knowledge about who they are in Christ, about how much God treasures them, and about the resources of the resurrected Christ available to them. It is one thing to teach people the principle that lifestyle changes come through changes in our thinking and that prayer is an important element in changing our thinking. It is another to guide them in prayer so these truths become infused in their sense of identity.

Many Christians today give intellectual assent to the facts and end results of what sanctification should look like, but do not have a transformed mind in their daily lives and relationships. They do not know how to walk out the process of taking God's truth from intellectual cognitive assent to become heart beliefs – passionate convictions. Nor are they good at getting rid of dysfunctional ingrained beliefs. This book lays out specific steps to accomplish these things, explaining how and what to pray, what to speak and when to keep silent, how to respond, how to facilitate an individual listening to God, and how to reflect on the present and past. The clarity with which Jean writes reflects her spiritual maturity, emotional sensitivity, and many years of experience with numerous people in various situations. This manual is a wealth of wisdom.

Another amazing aspect of the book is extensive applications to the common issues where dysfunctional thinking is rampant in our world today. The testimonies and dialogues provide clear, practical illustrations, showing how to apply the principles of Wholeness Prayer in ministry situations.

This book also expresses a healthy balance on spiritual warfare. It recognizes and deals with Satan's influence and attacks, but avoids the pitfalls of blaming all problems on the devil and claiming an immediate cure while the individual remains passive. Jean recognizes that in many situations transformation may involve a process, initiated by Wholeness Prayer ministry and walked out in daily life.

Every church would benefit greatly from having a team of people trained to do Wholeness Prayer ministry.

> ~ **John Ault, M. Div.**, Senior Pastor Emeritus,
> New Hope Community Church, Potsdam, NY

Preface

Ask and it will be given to you; seek and you will find;
knock and the door will be opened to you.
For everyone who asks receives; the one who seeks finds;
and to the one who knocks, the door will be opened.
~Matthew 7:7-8 (NIV)

I see life through the lens of friendship. Even years before I began using Wholeness Prayer, people would often share their struggles with me. I would listen, care, and pray with them. Together we would ask God to heal hurts, bring truth, and transform perspectives. After praying, all too often they would leave with their struggles still intact. Our experiences seemed to lack the resurrection power of the New Testament.

In 2000, I asked Dr. David Wickstrom, a clinical psychologist, what tools might equip me to better help my friends with their needs. He gave me a list of ideas, many of which involved learning about the various struggles people face and helping them find healthy ways forward. The suggestion that appealed to me most was rooted in prayer: coming to God together with the person in need, and asking our Great Counselor to reveal root issues and bring breakthroughs.

As I learned more about finding release, through prayer, from emotional and spiritual stuck places, I began to understand how much fear had colored my own life. I started to see disconnects between my logical conclusions and how I responded emotionally. I identified things I "believed" at an emotional level that were inconsistent with biblical truth. Things like: "If I don't do everything right, something bad will happen" or "Life goes better when you're afraid." I had thought my patterns of behavior were normal, but I increasingly realized they weren't healthy.

I began to intentionally take my thoughts captive (2 Corinthians 10:5) and bring them to God, together with my emotions and actions. Then I asked God to speak to the root of these everyday issues. He increasingly brought light and truth into the darkened places of my perspective. My ability to connect with the truth of Scripture at a heart level increased, as did my hunger for God and His Word.

Previously, I had attempted to memorize verses about not being afraid, meditate on those Scriptures, and put them into practice. But these efforts hadn't changed my thought patterns or heart-level responses. When I shut my Bible, the truth relentlessly drifted away. This happened no matter how hard I tried to hold onto it or how desperately I longed for breakthroughs. During that season, God used some "hit the wall" experiences to bring greater freedom. For example, as I was recovering from pneumonia over three decades ago, He used Psalm 103 to powerfully show me the reality of His great love for *me*.

> *Bless the Lord, O my soul,*
> *And all that is within me, bless His holy name.*
> *Bless the Lord, O my soul, And forget none of His benefits;*
> *Who pardons all your iniquities, Who heals all your diseases;*
> *Who redeems your life from the pit,*
> *Who crowns you with lovingkindness and compassion;*
> *Who satisfies your years with good things,*
> *So that your youth is renewed like the eagle.*
> ~Psalm 103:1-5 (NASB)

Almost from the beginning, I started applying Wholeness Prayer principles when praying with others. As I did, I increasingly saw God do miraculous things in their lives. He set them free where they'd been stuck spiritually or emotionally. When my friends shared their burdens with me, we prayed together and asked God to speak to the root of issues. More and more consistently He brought lasting Kingdom breakthroughs. Sometimes this happened in mere minutes, other times through multiple prayer sessions. Those I prayed with no longer left carrying the same struggles and burdens. They received God's truth at the root of their issues and became radiant. Together, we experienced the glorious New Testament power I'd longed for.

I began praying with more and more people and facilitating trainings. As I did so, God set free many who had formerly been held captive spiritually or emotionally. However, this freedom wasn't yet reaching most of the Indonesians I lived among, many of whom were functionally illiterate. I sought the best way to communicate these principles to them, so that they could be easily understood, applied, and multiplied. Materials I initially wrote were further honed through valuable feedback. A friend suggested the name *Wholeness Prayer,* as this type of interactive prayer with God results in increased wholeness in the lives of those touched by it.

Over the years, I've read multiple books on spiritual and emotional healing, counseling, change theory, and internal motivation. I've studied works on leadership, relational styles, hearing God, codependency, addictions, trauma, abuse, dissociative identity disorder (DID), and deliverance ministry. I've gleaned valuable insights from authors such as Jim Wilder, Tim Clinton, Henry Cloud, John Townsend, Daniel Goleman, Steven M Covey, Kerry Patterson, John Kotter, Dan Cohen, Melody Beattie, Ed Murphy, Alfred Davis, Tom and Diane Hawkins, Ed Smith, Leanne Payne, Derek Prince, and Neil Anderson. I've tested their contributions by the Word of God and discarded ideas for which I couldn't find a biblical foundation. In the process, I've found keys to unlock doors of unforgiveness, bitterness, trauma, abuse, codependency, old thought patterns, and more. I'm grateful to God for those who've gone before me and to all who are journeying together with me. I'm thankful that God is our healer. To Him be the glory.

Introduction

God is using Wholeness Prayer in powerful ways to set spiritual and emotional captives free. Thousands from over 15 countries[1], in all six inhabited continents, are experiencing lasting victory.

Wholeness Prayer empowers followers of Christ to pray for people struggling spiritually or emotionally. This involves inviting God to speak directly to the person being prayed for at the root of the issues they're facing. The five main steps (5 R's) involved in Wholeness Prayer are
  (1) *Recognize:* Identify (take captive) your negative feelings, thoughts, and/or actions.
  (2) *Recent:* Bring these to God and ask Him to reveal a related recent memory.
  (3) *Root:* Ask God to reveal any root(s) – the first time (or pattern) when you thought, felt, and/or acted this way.
  (4) *Receive:* Receive His perspective – first at the root, if there is one.
  (5) *Renew:* Apply this perspective in everyday life.

This book has two goals: (1) Making the content of basic Wholeness Prayer trainings available to followers of Christ who have not attended a workshop, and to those who have attended a workshop and want to review the basic principles; (2) Going broader and deeper than the material presented in basic Wholeness Prayer workshops – giving further applications, additional biblical basis and representative examples, and multiple testimonies.

Together, Parts 1 and 2 give a basic overview of Wholeness Prayer. Designed to be worked through first, Part 1 focuses on general understanding and application of the 5 R's in Wholeness Prayer. Part 2 builds on this framework by introducing concrete keys that have proven helpful in addressing nine common issues.

Part 3 adds to this framework, offering ideas and keys useful for addressing additional situations. Part 4 looks at potential applications of Wholeness Prayer to multiple contexts. An epilogue suggests reflection questions for continuing to move forward in understanding, applying, and multiplying Wholeness Prayer. Appendix 1 consists of a two-page guide to facilitating a time of Wholeness Prayer. Appendix 2 gives links to other Wholeness Prayer resources, including the Simplified Version booklet presently being used in trainings around the world. Appendix 3 compiles keys for Wholeness Prayer presented throughout this book. Appendix 4 explores biblical foundations of wholeness.

In addition to personal testimonies, this book includes many *representative* experiences of people who have gained increased freedom through Wholeness Prayer. Identifying details have been changed as needed to protect confidentiality.

Becoming Whole is intentionally written for multiple audiences, including those for whom English is not their first language. The focus is on practical application, not theory. This book does not attempt to exhaustively define or analyze issues people struggle with. It aims to offer principles and keys that have helped bring Kingdom breakthroughs through prayer, as God interacts directly with the person being prayed for.

Becoming Whole intentionally uses "they/their/them" as first person singular pronouns instead of "he/his/him" and "she/hers/her." This helps avoid the trap of seeing Wholeness Prayer issues and keys as inherently more applicable to either the male or female gender. Although often seen as grammatically incorrect, the gender-neutral singular "they/their/them" is becoming increasingly common in English, with dictionaries like *Merriam Webster* and publications like *The New York Times* now recognizing it as a legitimate alternative to gender-specific singular pronouns. The 2011 NIV has also chosen to follow this pattern: Psalm 32:2, for example, reads, "Blessed is the one whose sin the LORD does not count against them and in whose spirit is no deceit."

Keys that have proven effective are included in each chapter and compiled at the end of the book. Page references throughout the book help the reader easily navigate between chapters and sections.

External links give easy access to more in-depth information on selected topics.

Tips for Using this Book

- Think of this book as guide to continually return to on your journey into Wholeness Prayer.
- The 5 R's and the guiding principle of "Follow Jesus" are the heart of Wholeness Prayer. Focus on internalizing those principles.
- Part 1 gives the foundation of Wholeness Prayer. Specific sections of Parts 2 & 3 will be most relevant in particular situations.
- As you become familiar with Wholeness Prayer, return regularly to the Table of Contents to see what sections would be good to revisit. Review relevant sections before going into times of prayer that seem likely to include those issues.
- Don't expect to memorize all of this content. Instead, familiarize yourself with the content and return to sections as the need arises. You will internalize sections as you bring together information with real-life contexts.
- Notice the role of three-way prayer (page 34) throughout Wholeness Prayer. As you read through specific sections, identify who is speaking and who is listening. You might want to color-code or highlight these in some way.
- Consider gathering a group of fellow learners to read through the text and practice Wholeness Prayer. You can learn much from God and one another as you explore together.

Part 1. Basic Wholeness Prayer

"God has done great things through Wholeness Prayer in Indonesia and elsewhere. It has borne fruit among Indonesians seeking to reach unreached people groups and among field workers from other nationalities (e.g. Philippines, USA). These field workers serve many nations, including but not limited to Indonesian unreached people groups. I've also been using Wholeness Prayer with several first-generation followers of Christ and their children.

Through Wholeness Prayer, I have seen God set people free from bitterness, sexual addiction, woundedness, trauma, rape, sexual abuse, pain, occult bondage, and more. Wholeness Prayer ministry is very valuable and God has used it far more than we expected and prayed for. All glory to our dear Lord!" ~L, Indonesia

Part 1 gives a general framework for Wholeness Prayer. Chapter 1 takes a brief look at the bigger picture – finding freedom and wholeness through Christ. Chapter 2 introduces the basic 5 R's of Wholeness Prayer, all of which are focused on the main goal: *following Jesus*. Chapter 3 includes scenarios illustrating the power of Wholeness Prayer in two situations. Chapter 4 covers basic Wholeness Prayer principles and guidelines. Chapter 5 gives ideas for overcoming hindrances that may be encountered during Wholeness Prayer.

Chapter 1. Finding Freedom

I am the Lord, I have called You in righteousness,
I will also hold You by the hand and watch over You,
And I will appoint You as a covenant to the people,
As a light to the nations, To open blind eyes,
To bring out prisoners from the dungeon
And those who dwell in darkness from the prison.
I am the Lord, that is My name;
I will not give My glory to another,
Nor My praise to graven images.
~Isaiah 42: 6-8 (NASB)

"A field worker serving in Papua, Indonesia felt he was not qualified to be in leadership because of false beliefs rooted in his past. Now he is the leader of a non-governmental organization which trains field workers for tent-making in Indonesia and abroad.

A leader of a non-governmental organization located in an unreached area of Indonesia felt so tired and burned out from interacting with her co-workers that she was ready to let go of her ministry and start elsewhere. After God encountered her through Wholeness Prayer, she gained perspective and renewed strength to persevere.

Two field workers who were served by Wholeness Prayer were later used by God to ignite a movement in a Sumatran unreached people group. Their encounter with God made them more effective and pulled down the internal barriers that had previously hindered their ministry." ~L, Indonesia

Our Heritage. As followers of Christ, we live in between the already and the not yet. We have already been set free from the power of sin (Romans 6:3-13). We've been rescued, redeemed, and forgiven (Colossians 1:13). We've received a new heart (Ezekiel 36:26). The Holy Spirit lives in us, and He loves to communicate with us (John 14:16-17, 26; 15:26; 16:13-15). We've been born into a living hope and given indescribable joy (1 Peter 1:3-9). We've been given a peace that passes understanding (Philippians 4:7).

In spite of this incredible heritage, our thought processes are not yet finished being transformed. We may have problems stemming from our heritage, from curses, or from choosing sin. We may believe things that aren't rooted in biblical truth, such as "I have to protect myself," "Anything that goes wrong is my fault," or "No one could ever love me."

We are engaged in spiritual warfare (Ephesians 6:12). In the midst of this, God is at work in us, transforming us into His image (2 Corinthians 3:18). We are called to join with God in this process. Matthew 12:33 (NIV) says, "Make a tree good and its fruit will be good, or make a tree bad and its fruit will be bad, for a tree is recognized by its fruit." If any of the fruit in our lives isn't good, we need healing at a root level.

Planting a field.

Behold, the sower went out to sow; and as he sowed, some seeds fell beside the road, and the birds came and ate them up. Others fell on the rocky places, where they did not have much soil; and immediately they sprang up, because they had no depth of soil. But when the sun had risen, they were scorched; and because they had no root, they withered away. Others fell among the thorns, and the thorns came up and choked them out. And others fell on the good soil and yielded a crop, some a hundredfold, some sixty, and some thirty. He who has ears, let him hear.
~Matthew 13:3b-9 (NASB)

Before a farmer plants crops in a field, he first clears and prepares the land. What would happen if the farmer only cut off the tops of the weeds filling the field, but left the roots intact? Any new seeds he sowed would be choked by the weeds. Similarly, if he sowed seeds by the side of the road, or in a field full of rocks or thorns, they would be unable to bear good fruit.

In a similar way, if the fields of our lives are full of weeds, how will new seeds take root and grow? If we struggle with unhealthy emotions, thoughts, or actions, the fields of our lives may still have unhealthy roots that need to be cleared away. Examples of these include unhealthy anger, unhealthy shame or fear, sin patterns, false beliefs, addictions, unresolved trauma, unforgiveness, and bitterness.

Reflection Questions
- What is presently growing in the field of your life?
- What good plants in the field of your life would you like to ask God to bless and make even more fruitful?
- What weeds, together with their roots, would you like to ask God to remove from the field of your life?
- What seeds would you like to ask God to plant and cause to grow and bear fruit in your life?

Chapter 2. The Basic Framework of Wholeness Prayer

The thief comes only to steal and kill and destroy;
I came that they may have life, and have it abundantly.
~John 10:10 (NASB)

"I graduated from college in 2007, and hit rock bottom. Anxiety and fear gripped me like never before. After clawing part of my way out of the pit through cognitive behavioral therapy, I was offered the opportunity to do Wholeness Prayer. Where standard therapy offered coping, Wholeness Prayer offered healing.

God spoke to me through a vision during Wholeness Prayer. I was in a prison cell, a dungeon. The door was open and the chains were broken, but I was cowering inside the cell. God spoke to me about the spiritual reality of the freedom I have in Christ that I was not embracing, and it was powerful.

God has continued to speak into and through my life with this vision, moving me into greater freedom each step of the way. He has even used my journey from captivity into freedom to empower me to lead others on the same path. He has revealed that He has the ability to redeem any part of our lives as we let Him use our greatest weaknesses for a demonstration of His strength. I believe God has blessed Wholeness Prayer as a true path to experiencing a fuller measure of His deep healing and abiding love." ~R

1. How Can We "Get Our Stuff Back"?

One day when my children were small, I was packed with them into a public transportation van in Bandung, Indonesia, a city of over three million people. The person sitting scrunched next to me took advantage of the crowded van. He stealthily slit my purse and stole my house keys. I didn't realize what had happened until after he had exited the van. Once I knew I'd been robbed, I was furious. I wanted my keys back!

We can be robbed in a variety of ways, including spiritually and emotionally (e.g. of our peace, joy, or hope). Once we realize we've been robbed, we can use the following principles to "get our stuff back." This is where Wholeness Prayer comes in.

2. The Wholeness Prayer Framework

Follow Jesus. The main Wholeness Prayer principle is *Follow Jesus*. He is our rescuer. He trains us for battle and gives us victory, together with Him (Psalm 18:31-42).

Throughout the Wholeness Prayer process, we keep our prayers short, then wait for God to speak directly to the person being prayed for. As they share as much of what He reveals[2] as they desire, we look for the next thing to bring to God in prayer.

Opening Prayer. We begin with an opening prayer. In that prayer, we invite God to lead the Wholeness Prayer time and accomplish all He desires through it. We ask for His protection and we bind the evil one and forbid him to interfere, in Jesus' name.

Recognize. The first basic step in the 5 R's of Wholeness Prayer is for God to help the person being prayed for to identify (take captive) their negative feelings, thoughts, and actions (2 Corinthians 10: 5). We ask God to reveal to them any ways in which they've been robbed, and to help them quickly identify those (e.g. lost joy, negative emotions, false beliefs, someone to forgive, unconfessed sin, unhealthy fear, shame or anger).

During a Wholeness Prayer time, after praying an opening prayer, we might simply pray, "Lord God, please reveal to [*the person being prayed for*] anything within them that would be good to pray through now." We then wait to see what comes to their mind.

Recent. The second basic step is to bring to God the negative thoughts, feelings or actions the person being prayed for desires to pray through at this time. We then ask Him to reveal a related recent memory.

During a Wholeness Prayer time, we thank God for what He has helped the person being prayed for to recognize in the previous step. Then we might pray, "Lord God, please reveal to [*the person being prayed for*] a recent time when they felt, thought and/or acted this way."

This memory[3] is usually fairly easy for the person to access. If they feel stuck, we might ask God to show them any reason why they might not *want* to remember. If nothing comes to the person's mind, it's often helpful to ask them what thought *first* came into their mind during the prayer time. Sometimes a thought has come to mind but gets overlooked. In some other cases, people have beliefs that act like sentinels to keep them from the healing process. These might be something like: "This won't work," or "I don't want to remember the past." In that case, assuming the person is willing, this sentinel belief is the next thing to take captive and bring to God in prayer.

Once the recent memory (or sentinel belief) is identified, we thank God for this. Then we pray, "Lord God, in this recent memory please reveal to [*the person being prayed for*] any thoughts, feelings and/or actions that are important for them to know now, so that they can bring them back to You in prayer."

If no feelings have yet been revealed, we might pray, "God, would You please reveal any underlying emotions involved?"

Root. After identifying feelings, beliefs and actions in the recent memory, the next step is to ask God to reveal any roots. This would be the *first* time (or pattern) when the person being prayed for thought, felt, and/or acted this way – or it might be a generational pattern. Usually the recent memory is not the root. In some cases, including trauma, the recent memory may also be the root.

During a Wholeness Prayer time, we thank God for what He has revealed related to the recent memory. Then we might pray, "Lord God, please help [*the person being prayed for*] to think and feel as much as you want them to of what they were thinking and feeling in this recent memory. As they do, please reveal to them the first time they thought, felt, or acted this way, and/or if this has been a pattern in their life." If it is a pattern, God may (or may not) bring to mind one or more representative memories.

Once the root memory (or pattern) is identified, we thank God for this. We then pray, "Lord God, in this first memory (or pattern), please reveal to [*the person being prayed for*] any thoughts, feelings, and/or actions that they need to know so that we can bring them back to You in prayer.

Part of what is revealed may be unhealthy ways in which the person reacted in the situation. Processing these might include working through any sin to confess (page 99), vows (page 132), judgments (page 139), or curses (page 134) they made, emotional wounds (page 67), unforgiveness (page 101), unhealthy patterns they've been living in (page 159), or counterfeit desires they've chosen to follow (page 143). There may also be unpleasant emotions based on truth (page 71), such as grief and loss (page 93).

Note: If the recent or root memory involves a sequence of events (such as is common with trauma), work through these events in chronological order, starting with the earliest one. For each significant event in the sequence that does not yet feel peaceful, ask God to reveal key feelings and false beliefs involved. Ask Him to then reveal His truth (first in an earlier root memory, if there is one).

Receive. After feelings, beliefs and actions are identified in the root memory (or pattern), the next step is for the person to receive God's perspective in this root memory (or pattern).

During a Wholeness Prayer time, we thank God for what He has revealed related to the root memory (or pattern). Then we might pray, "Lord God, as [*the person being prayed for*] thinks and feels as much as You want them to of what they were thinking and feeling in this memory, please reveal Your perspective." (If someone has experienced abuse, it generally works much better if the person being prayed for prays aloud at this point. If they are ready to do so, they can invite God to speak into the root memory.)

As the person shares as much as they desire of what they feel God is revealing, test this to see if it aligns with biblical truth. If it doesn't, take it captive and ask God to reveal the first time the person felt this way. Follow Jesus to receive truth, then return to working through the root memory.[4]

Once the person has received God's perspective in the root memory (or pattern), we thank God for this. We then pray "Lord God, please reveal to [*the person being prayed for*] if there is anything remaining in this memory that doesn't yet feel peaceful."

Continue to pray through the issues that emerge until the root memory (or pattern) is peaceful. It may contain a variety of issues that need to be prayed through. Keys for common issues can be found in Parts 2 and 3 of this book.

You may find it helpful to ask God to show the person anything He would like to give them (e.g. blessing, comfort, sense of His love, purity) in place of the thing they are surrendering to Him (e.g. false belief, unhealthy vow, unhealthy anger, unforgiveness, bitterness, shame).

Renew. The next step is to ask God to show the person being prayed for how they can apply this perspective in everyday life. As Jesus reveals truth to correct each false belief, that truth changes how the person interprets the original memory and any similar situations in their past. It also impacts any similar situations that may arise in the future.

During a Wholeness Prayer time, we thank God for what He has revealed related to the root memory (or pattern). Then we might pray, "Lord God, please show [*the person being prayed for*] how the truth You've revealed applies (or could have applied) in this root memory (or pattern)."

Once this is revealed, we thank God for this. Then we pray "Lord God, please show [*the person being prayed for*] how the truth You've revealed applies (or could have applied) in the recent memory.

After this is revealed, we thank God for this. Then we pray "Lord God, please show [*the person being prayed for*] how the truth You've revealed applies to their life now and for the future."

We ask God to help the person being prayed for to consistently walk in this new pattern. We invite Him to show them how to return to walking victoriously in the new pattern if they begin to fall back into the old pattern. We encourage them to thank God for what He's done and to rejoice in these victories.

Closing Prayer. Before closing in prayer, we ask God to bring to mind anything else He'd like us to pray through. If something else comes to the person's mind, we work through those things (as time allows), using the same pattern of Wholeness Prayer. After that, we thank God for all He's done during the prayer time and ask Him to help the person apply His truth in their daily lives. We also ask Him to send away any evil spirits connected with the issues that have been prayed through: to send them wherever He desires – never to return – and to protect all involved. And we ask Jesus to fill any empty places in the person with Himself. We also ask Him to remind the person of the new path He has revealed each time they encounter a similar situation, and to help them consistently choose this new path.

Follow up. After the prayer time is over, we may ask the person if there's anything else they'd like to share with us about what God did during the prayer time. We encourage them to share, with others whom they trust, what God has done. We also encourage them to meditate on related Scriptures, to follow through with any follow-up actions God has revealed, and to continue to thank God for His victories. These steps help the new pattern to grow in stability and the person to grow in joy and intimacy with Christ.

3. A Diagram of the Wholeness Prayer Process

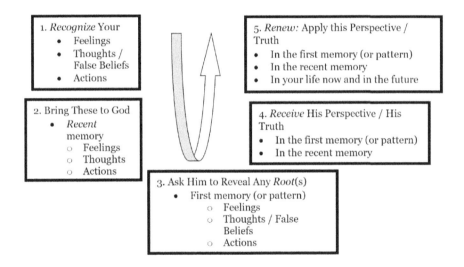

A guide to facilitating a time of Wholeness Prayer is included in Appendix 1.

Keys
- Recognize
- Recent
- Root
- Receive
- Renew

Chapter 3. Representative Scenarios

This chapter includes dialogues often used during Wholeness Prayer trainings to contrast the use or absence of basic Wholeness Prayer steps. Each set of scenarios begins with the same situation, then illustrates what Wholeness Prayer is and what it is *not*. Questions are included for reflection.

Scenario 1: Sam and Mike

What Wholeness Prayer Is *Not*

Sam (sharing with his accountability partner Mike):
I yelled at my teammate, Jim, again today. I know I shouldn't yell at him, but he's so irresponsible. I remember you shared those Bible verses with me last week - Colossians 3:12-14[5]. I memorized them: "Therefore, as God's chosen people, holy and dearly loved, clothe yourselves with compassion, kindness, humility, gentleness, and patience. Bear with each other and forgive whatever grievances you may have against one another. Forgive as the Lord forgave you. And over all these virtues put on love, which binds them all together in perfect unity." And I really tried to apply them.
But yesterday Jim got busy with his email and forgot to meet Yuhei, our national ministry partner, again. Yuhei called me because he couldn't get through to Jim. Yuhei said he feels like Jim doesn't really care about him or the ministry. When I finally got ahold of Jim, I said a lot of harsh things to him.

Mike: I noticed in your story that you called Jim irresponsible. It's not good to label someone that way.

Sam, hanging his head in shame: I know you're right. You've told me that before. But he is irresponsible. And he just won't change.

Mike: Let's pray and ask God to give you more patience. God, please help Sam to be more patient with Jim. Amen.

Reflection Questions
- If you were in Sam's position, how might you feel afterward?
- If you were in Mike's position, how might you feel afterward?
- Have you ever been in a situation similar to Sam's? Or to Mike's? If so, how did you feel?
- What issues do you think needed to be addressed in this situation with Sam?

What Wholeness Prayer Is

Sam (sharing with his accountability partner Mike):
I yelled at my teammate, Jim, again today. I know I shouldn't yell at him, but he's so irresponsible. I remember you shared those Bible verses with me last week - Colossians 3:12-14[6]. I memorized them: "Therefore, as God's chosen people, holy and dearly loved, clothe yourselves with compassion, kindness, humility, gentleness, and patience. Bear with each other and forgive whatever grievances you may have against one another. Forgive as the Lord forgave you. And over all these virtues put on love, which binds them all together in perfect unity." And I really tried to apply them.
But yesterday Jim got busy with his email and forgot to meet Yuhei, our national ministry partner, again. Yuhei called me because he couldn't get through to Jim. Yuhei said he feels like Jim doesn't really care about him or the ministry. When I finally got ahold of Jim, I said a lot of harsh things to him.

Mike: That sounds hard. Would you like to pray about this situation together?

Sam: Sure, that sounds good.

Mike: If it's okay with you, I'd like to pray using Wholeness Prayer principles. I've just been learning about them and I think they might be useful in this situation.

Sam: What's Wholeness Prayer?

Mike: There are 5 basic steps: (1) Recognize: With God's help, you identify and take captive negative feelings, thoughts, and actions; (2) Recent: We bring these to God and ask Him to reveal a related recent memory; (3) Root: We ask God to reveal any root(s) – the first time (or pattern) when you thought, felt, and/or acted this way; (4) Receive: You receive God's perspective - first at the root, if there is one; and (5) Renew: You apply this perspective in your everyday life.
I would focus on praying aloud and I'd ask God to speak directly to you. You'd focus on listening, and on whatever's going on inside you, including your thoughts and emotions. You can tell me as much as you want to about what He reveals, then I'll pray again. Does that sound okay?

Sam: Yes.

Mike: God, we thank You that we can come to You with all of our problems and struggles. We bring to You now Sam's situation with Jim. We ask that You lead our prayer time, and accomplish all You want to through this time. We ask that You bring to Sam's mind anything that You want him to remember, and that You reveal to him all that You want to reveal.
Please fill this place and each of us with Yourself, and surround us with Your protection. We ask that You move aside any powers or principalities who seek to interfere with this prayer time. In the name of Jesus, we bind any evil spirits who seek to interfere, and command them to stand aside as You work. We thank You for all that You're going to do.
Lord, we ask that You bring to Sam's mind right now whatever You want him to remember about today's situation with Jim.

Sam [*after about 3 seconds*]: I'm remembering how angry I felt at Jim.

Mike: God, I pray You'd help Sam to remember how he felt right before he got angry. Please especially show him if he felt any fear, frustration, shame, or hurt.

Sam: I felt really frustrated because Jim forgot to meet Yuhei. And afraid that Yuhei would leave the ministry.

Mike: God, we thank You for showing Sam that he was feeling frustrated and afraid. I ask that You help him to feel his frustration and fear as much as You want him to for a moment, and, as he does, please show him the first time he felt this way.

Sam: Wow, this is weird! I haven't thought of this in a long time! When I was twelve I was working on a project in the backyard. My dad came out to look at it, then took over. He said I never did things right. I felt frustrated, ashamed, and afraid that I could never please him. I vowed then that I would please him even if it killed me. And that I would always succeed in anything I did.

Mike: God, we thank You for revealing this memory to Sam. Please show him anything else in this memory that's important for us to know.

Sam: I felt like I had to do things "right" to be loved.

Mike: God, we come to You with all these things. Please help Sam to think and feel as much as You want him to in this memory right now of his fear, his frustration, and his feeling that he had to do things "right" to be loved. [*Wait about 5 seconds.*] As You do, please show Your perspective in this place.

Sam [*after about 5 seconds*]: God says that He loves me. And that it's not because I succeed at some project - but all the time, even when I fail. He was there with me when my dad said I never did things right. He says it's not true. And that I'm not alone. I've always felt so alone – like I had to do everything myself. But I can partner with God, my help and my strength. This is what I choose. Like Philippians 4:13 says: "*I can do all things through Him who strengthens me.*"7 I can do whatever He wants by His power. He's saying that I truly "succeed" when I trust and surrender, not when I push for what I want or think is best.

Mike: God, we thank You that You were there, and that You love Sam all the time. Thank You that he's not alone. Please continue to reveal Your perspective.

Sam: I think God wants me to give up the vow I made to always succeed. He wants me to trust Him with the results of what I do, not try to control things myself.

Mike: Would you like to tell God that now?

Sam: Yes. Dear God, I release to You the vow I made when I was twelve to always succeed. I choose to trust You with my life, and with the results of what I do. Please help me to learn how to walk in this new way. Amen.

Mike: God, we thank You that Sam has given You this vow. We ask You to bless this new pattern, and to show us if there's anything else You'd like to reveal to Sam regarding this memory.

Sam: I think I need to forgive my dad for this. I've worked through forgiving him for lots of things, but I haven't yet forgiven him for this.

Mike: God, we thank You for revealing this to Sam. Would You please show him if he can release this to You and forgive his dad for this, or if there's anything to pray through first?

Sam: I feel ready to release it. God, I release this hurt to You. Please forgive my dad for this, and bless him. Please help him to be all You want him to be. Thank You. In Jesus' name, Amen.

Mike: God, we thank You for this. Please show us if there's anything else You'd like us to pray about now, related to this memory, or to Jim.

Sam: I need to forgive Jim but I feel stuck.

Mike: God, we thank You for showing Sam his need to forgive Jim. Will You please reveal to him now any reservations he has about forgiving Jim?

Sam: I think I feel like Jim will "get away with" hurting Yuhei if I forgive him. But even as I say that, I'm realizing that God can take care of this. So I feel ready to forgive Jim.
God, I choose now to release Jim from this offense. Will You please take care of this, and help both Jim and me to grow? And will You please bless and comfort Yuhei, and show me what my part is, if any, for follow-up? [*Wait a few seconds.*] I think God wants me to ask Jim's forgiveness for yelling at him. I'll plan to do that tonight. I also think God wants me to talk with Jim about the pattern of him forgetting things. But I don't know how to do that.

Mike: How about we close in prayer, then talk about that?

Sam: That sounds good.

Mike: God, we thank You for all You've done during this prayer time. We exalt Your name and ask that Your Kingdom come and Your will be done, in our lives as it is in Heaven.
In the name of Jesus, we bind any demonic powers that were connected to any of these issues, and command that they go now to the place Jesus sends them, and never return.
God, we ask that You fill every empty place in us with Yourself and protect us by Your power. Please especially bless the places in Sam that You've healed today. Please help Sam to live in the truth that You've revealed to him, and apply this truth in his life. Please help him to continually catch any negative thoughts, feelings, or actions; pray through any root causes; get your perspective; and apply it in his life and to his relationships. Please help him to keep growing in intimacy with You. Thank You that You've brought us out of darkness into Your marvelous light, that You love to walk with us, and that You transform our minds. Please continue Your healing in us. We give You all the praise and honor and glory. In Jesus' name, Amen.

Reflection Questions
- If you were in Sam's position, how might you feel afterward?
- If you were in Mike's position, how might you feel afterward?
- How did you see God at work in this prayer time?

Scenario 2: Diane and Marie

Scenario *not* using Wholeness Prayer principles

Diane: I dropped by Sue's house yesterday with a special cake for her. She took the package and said thanks, and we talked on her porch for a few minutes. Then she said she had to go. I'm very angry at her! I spent a lot of time making that cake for her and she didn't have time to even talk to me! I was so angry last night that I couldn't sleep.

Marie: I noticed in your story that you're angry. Did you let the sun go down on your anger?

Diane: Yes. I know I shouldn't do that. You've told me that before. But she made me so angry!

Marie: Let's pray and ask God to help you obey His Word. God, please help Diane not to let the sun go down on her anger. Amen.

Reflection Questions
- If you were in Diane's position, how might you feel afterward?
- If you were in Marie's position, how might you feel afterward?
- Have you ever been in a situation similar to Diane's? Or to Marie's? If so, how did you feel?
- What issues do you think needed to be addressed in this situation with Diane?

Part 1 of a Wholeness Prayer time with Diane

Diane: I dropped by Sue's house yesterday with a special cake for her. She took the package and said thanks, and we talked on her porch for a few minutes. Then she said she had to go. I'm very angry at her! I spent a lot of time making that cake for her and she didn't have time to even talk to me! I was so angry last night that I couldn't sleep.

Marie: That sounds hard. Would you like to pray about this situation together?

Diane: Okay, that sounds good.

Marie: If it's okay with you, I'd like to pray using 3-way prayer: I'll pray a brief opening prayer. Then I'll ask God to reveal something to you. Then you tell me as much as you want to about what He reveals, then I'll pray again. You focus on *listening* to God and on what's going on in your mind. You don't need to figure out what to pray. Does that sound okay to you?

Diane: Sure.

Marie: God, we thank You that we can come to You with all of our problems and struggles. We come before You now with Diane's situation with Sue. We ask You to lead our prayer time, and to accomplish all You want to through this time. We ask You to bring to Diane's mind anything that You want her to remember, and to reveal to her all that You desire.
Please fill this place and each of us with Yourself, and surround us with Your protection. We ask You to move aside any powers or principalities who would seek to interfere with this prayer time. In the name of Jesus, we bind any evil spirits who would seek to interfere, and command them to stand aside as You work. We thank You for all that You're going to do. We love You God. Please help us to love You more.
Lord, we ask You to bring to Diane's mind right now whatever You want her to remember about yesterday's situation with Sue.

Diane [*after about 15 seconds*]: I remember being really excited about giving the cake to Sue. All the time I was making it, I was thinking about how excited she'd be to receive it. She's told me often how much she loves my chocolate cake. When she wasn't excited, I felt very angry.

Marie: God, we thank You for this special present that Diane made for Sue. We bring before You her excitement about bringing the cake to Sue, and ask that You show her how she felt when it seemed that Sue didn't receive the cake with the excitement she had hoped for. Please show Diane how she felt just before she got angry – maybe hurt or frustrated or afraid or ashamed.

Diane [*after about 15 seconds*]: I felt disappointed because I wanted her to love the cake - and because I wanted to spend time with her. I felt hurt because I did all that work for her and she didn't have time for me. I felt frustrated because she didn't even look in the box. I also felt afraid because I wondered if Sue doesn't really like me as much as I'd thought.

Marie: God, we thank You for revealing these things to Diane. We ask that You'd help her to feel as much as You want her to – for a moment in Your presence – how she was feeling in this situation with Sue. [W*ait about 15 seconds.*]
God, as Diane thinks and feels as much of these things as You want her to, please show her the first time she felt this way. Please reveal to her if earlier in her life there was a similar situation, or a pattern of feeling this way. [*Wait about 20 seconds.*]

Diane: I often felt those things with my mother as I was growing up and I still often feel that way now. It's been a pattern in my life.

Marie: God, we thank You for revealing this pattern to Diane. If there's a significant memory (or group of memories) that You want to bring to mind where Diane felt this way, I pray that You bring those to her mind now. Otherwise we bring You the pattern as a whole. [*Wait about 15 seconds.*]

Please help Diane to think and feel now as much as You want her to of how she felt in these memories with her mom. [*Wait about 10 seconds.*]
As Diane thinks and feels for a moment in Your presence what she was thinking and feeling at those times, I ask You to reveal Your perspective to her. Please show her where You were and reveal Your truth. [*Wait about 20 seconds.*]

Diane: God showed me that I also felt very alone when I was growing up. My mom would often make fun of me in front of my friends, especially if I tried to do something nice for one of them. Then God showed me that He was with me. And He said that He's always been with me and always will be. I don't have to be afraid that people won't like me, because He loves me and He'll take care of me.

Marie: God, we thank You for revealing this to Diane. We thank You that you chose her before the foundation of the world, that You love her with an everlasting love, and that You will never leave her or forsake her. [*Wait about 5 seconds.*]
Lord, we pray that You will show Diane whether this place feels peaceful now or whether there's anything that is not yet worked through.

Diane: I feel sad about the wasted years of my life. I have a lot of disappointments that I'm carrying. And God is showing me that I need to forgive my mother.
Marie: God, we want to lift up before You Diane's sadness about the years that feel wasted. We thank You that You said in Isaiah 53:4 that You carried all of our griefs and sorrows on the cross. Please help Diane to feel as much of the sadness now as You want her to – for a moment in Your presence. [*Wait about 10 seconds.*]
Lord, as Diane feels this pain, sadness, and disappointment, we ask that You come and carry it. Please help her to release this burden to You. Thank You for dying on the cross, for carrying our pain and sorrows, and for Your resurrection power that's at work in our lives. [*Wait about 10 seconds.*]
Diane, how are you feeling?

Diane: I feel more peaceful, but like I really need to forgive my mother. But I've tried before and feel stuck.

Marie: Would it be okay if we close for now, then pray more about this later?

Diane: Yes, that sounds good.

Marie: God, thank You for all You've done during this prayer time. Thank You for speaking to Diane's heart and carrying her pain and sorrow. We ask You to seal the healing You've done, and help Diane apply these truths in her life. Please also help her to soon forgive her mother. Please protect any yet unhealed places within her, and speed the day of their healing.
In the name of Jesus, we bind any demonic powers that were connected to anything we've addressed during this prayer time, and command that they go now to the place Jesus sends them, and never return. God, please pour out Your Spirit on us, and protect us by Your power. Help us to see ourselves as You see us, and to see You as You are. We give You ourselves. Be glorified in us. In Jesus' name, Amen.

Part 2 of a Wholeness Prayer time with Diane

Marie: God, we thank You for bringing us together again. We come before You with thanksgiving for what You've already done and for what You're going to do. We invite You to lead this prayer time, and to accomplish all You desire. Please protect us by Your power, and move aside any powers and principalities who might seek to interfere. We bind the evil one in Your name, and command him to stand aside while You work.
God, please show us whether this is the time to pursue Diane forgiving her mother, or whether there is anything else to pray through first.

Diane: There isn't anything else I'm aware of right now. I would like to work on forgiving my mother.

Marie: Lord, we bring before You Diane's desire to forgive her mother. I pray that You'll help Diane to see her mother through Your eyes. Please help her to separate who You made her mother to be, with all her strengths and gifts, from her mother's sin, woundedness, and weaknesses. [*Wait about 10 seconds.*]
Please show Diane what specific things she needs to forgive her mother for.

Diane [*after about 10 seconds*]: I need to forgive my mom for saying things like "You'll never amount to anything." "Why are you so stupid?" and "Why are you always so slow?" Also for not having time for me. And for favoring my brother.

Marie: Lord, we thank You for revealing these things to Diane. For whichever thing You want to address first, please bring to Diane's mind the first time or a representative time this happened. [*Wait about 5 seconds.*]
Diane: I was working on my math homework and my mom said I was too slow. Then she said I'd never amount to anything and that I was stupid. She also asked me why I wasn't smart like my brother.

Marie: Lord, thank You for bringing this memory to Diane's mind. Please show her whatever she needs to know, regarding what she was thinking and feeling when her mom said these things.

Diane [*after about 10 seconds*]: I felt ashamed, not valued, and insignificant.

Marie: God, please help Diane to think and feel right now as much as You want her to of what she was thinking and feeling in this memory. [*Wait about 5 seconds.*]
Lord, as Diane thinks and feels this, please reveal Your perspective in this memory.

Diane: God was there and He was crying for my pain. He said that the hurtful things my mom said to me aren't true. Actually my mom was afraid that people would see how inadequate *she* felt. He said that my mom was feeling ashamed, not valued and insignificant. He reminded me that for years she has felt embarrassed because she feels slow at math and stupid. I remember her telling me that her mom used to ridicule her.
God said that He wants to carry my pain and my shame. He held out His arms and I ran to Him. He said that I'm of great value to Him. He wants to walk with me every moment. I can always run to Him.
I'm so sorry for my mom's pain. I feel I can forgive her now for saying those things.

Marie: God, we thank You for this! Thank You that You love Diane so much that You died for her, so that she could be set free.
Please show Diane which things she's ready to forgive her mom for now, and which, if any, still feel hard to release to You.

Diane: I think I can release them all now. God's showing me that my mom was very wounded herself and didn't know how to connect with me. I feel sad about that, but I can forgive my mom for it. I think she favored my brother because he was quick at math. I have other things that I do well. More importantly, God loves me.

Marie: Would you like to pray a prayer of forgiveness for your mom now?

Diane: Yes. God, I choose to forgive my mom for all these things – as well as for not being the perfect mom I thought she should be. She's wounded too. Please bless her and help her to grow in You, and become who You created her to be. Thank You that she knows You.

Marie: God, we thank You that Diane has forgiven her mom for these things. If other things come up that she needs to forgive her mom for, please help her to do that.
God, please help Diane feel as much as You want her to now of the sadness she feels about her mom's woundedness and not knowing how to connect with her. [*Wait about 5 seconds.*]
As Diane feels this sadness, please come and carry this for her, and help her to give You her burden. [*Wait about 15 seconds.*]
Diane, how do you feel?

Diane: I feel peaceful.

Marie: God, we thank You for carrying this burden. Please fill Diane with Yourself, and with Your joy. Please deepen her intimacy with You day by day.
God, I pray You'll show Diane how what You've spoken relates to the situation with Sue. And whether Diane needs to forgive Sue.

Diane: God's showing me that I've been wanting Sue to always be there for me – like my mom couldn't be. Sue has a family and works. She can't be there for me all the time, but God can. I've been unreasonable in my expectations with Sue. I need to release her from being for me what my mom couldn't be for me. I don't think I need to forgive her, because she really didn't do anything wrong. She didn't know I was coming over.
God, I release Sue from being my mom for me. Help me to receive from You all that I need.

Marie: God, thank You for giving Diane Your perspective and helping her to release Sue. Thank You that You've given Diane all she needs for life and godliness. Please show us if there's anything else You'd like us to pray through now.

Diane: I feel peaceful. I don't think there's anything else right now.

Marie: God, we thank You for all You've done during this prayer time. We exalt Your name and ask that Your Kingdom come and Your will be done, in our lives as it is in Heaven.
In the name of Jesus, we bind any demonic powers that were connected to these issues, and command that they go now to the place Jesus sends them, and never return.
God, we ask that You fill every empty place in us with Yourself and protect us by Your power. Please especially bless the places in Diane that You've healed today, and help her to access these healed memories when she chooses to. Please help Diane to live in the truth that You've revealed to her, and apply this truth in her life. Please help Diane to continually recognize any negative thoughts, feelings, or actions and pray through any root causes. Please help her receive Your perspective, and apply it in her life and relationships.
Please help Diane to keep growing in intimacy with You. Thank You that You've brought us out of darkness into Your marvelous light, that You love to walk with us, and that You transform our minds. Please continue Your healing in us. We give You all the praise and honor and glory. In Jesus' name, Amen.

Result. Diane feels released. When she returns home, she finds that Sue has called. Diane calls her back and Sue joyfully thanks her for the cake. Diane thanks God for the good resolution. Diane grows in being a better friend and not putting unreasonable expectations on Sue. She also grows in intimacy with God, and in joy.

Reflection Questions
- If you were in Diane's position, how might you feel afterward?
- If you were in Marie's position, how might you feel afterward?
- How did you see God at work during this prayer time?

Chapter 4. Basic Principles and Guidelines

"As I prayed through some things, God brought to mind an experience I had while working in an office a few years ago. I had been whistling a song in the hallway and in my office. (I know it's impolite to whistle inside a building, and probably unprofessional, too.)

One day a coworker with a very imposing stature and voice was fed up with my whistling. He came to my office and stood in the doorway. I sensed a presence there but didn't pay any attention at first. He didn't do anything to get my attention. After a while, I realized he was still there. The situation started to feel a bit threatening.

When I looked, I saw him filling my doorway. He had an intense look on his face. I think I asked him if I could help him. He looked as if it was all he could do not to walk inside my office and strangle me. He gritted his teeth and said, 'Would you PLEEEEEASE stop that whistling?'

It was the strangest feeling. I thought if that he could have stopped me from ever whistling again in that moment, he might have. I guess I must have felt some fear, as well as a bit of embarrassment. My whistling was often an involuntary, joyful thing. Sometimes I didn't even consciously know I was whistling.

I also felt disturbed because he told me after he was already enraged. He seemed ready to almost hurt me. Yet he hadn't said anything about my whistling before. (I guess he was trying to be gracious about this habit of mine that caused him distress. He later told me he has tinnitus that is very much set off by high-pitched sounds. He must have suffered a long time because I really did whistle a lot back then!)

I remembered this moment and was talking with God about it. Then I saw Jesus standing in the doorway between us. He was blocking my coworker from entering and protecting me from my coworker's wrath. Wow!

Thank you for praying with me and helping me learn to pray in this way." ~M

God often brings Kingdom breakthroughs during Wholeness Prayer. He does this by speaking to the person being prayed for at the root of the issues involved.

Wholeness Prayer principles are different from *immediately* offering advice, giving direction, or teaching biblical principles. These principles work well alongside counseling and the usual pattern of intercessory prayer. They directly contrast with downplaying or denying our issues, or trying to overcome them ourselves instead of bringing them to God.

In Wholeness Prayer, we ask God to speak directly to the person being prayed for at their point of need. The goal is for the person being prayed for to recognize and bring to God troublesome thoughts, feelings and actions. They can then get His perspective at the root of related issues, and live in this truth and freedom.

Clarify your Role. If you are not certified as a counselor or mental health provider, let the person you're praying with know this before you begin facilitating a Wholeness Prayer session with them.

3-way Conversation. When praying for another person using Wholeness Prayer principles, we engage in a 3-way conversation with God. He leads the process. We surrender the prayer time and its results to Him.

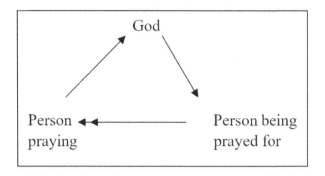

The person being prayed for focuses on listening to what God is revealing to them, and to their thoughts and feelings. They tell the person praying for them as much as they want to of: (1) what God is doing, (2) what thoughts and emotions they are feeling in a memory, and (3) what happened in the memory.

The person facilitating the prayer time seeks to listen well to God and to the person being prayed for. They also aim to discern where the person being prayed for currently is in the process and what might be good to pray next. They mainly pray aloud to God and listen to the person being prayed for. They refrain from inserting personal input into the process. They may find it helpful to silently ask God questions such as these when praying for someone: "Where are we at present in this process?", "What keys might be helpful to use now?", or "What might be a good thing to bring to You in prayer now?"

The person being prayed for rarely prays aloud. (Actively deciding what to next pray aloud can make it more challenging for the person to focus on listening to and receiving from God.) However, there are times when it is important for them to do so. Examples include decisions (e.g. forgiving someone or choosing something) and requests (e.g. asking God to forgive, bless, cancel or restore something). They also occasionally benefit from praying aloud to pour out their heart to God regarding emotions in a memory (although most often, people do this without praying aloud).

When praying with someone, notice their facial expressions and body language. This can help you know when they are still processing and when they might be ready to share with you. It can also give you clues as to when they might be stuck in the process. Often people will open their eyes or look up when they have had enough time to quietly listen and receive from God.

Each time you ask God to reveal something to the person, wait for approximately 10-15 seconds. (This will vary; some people will benefit from longer times of silent waiting on God.) Then, if they haven't shared anything, ask them if anything has come to mind. If something has come to mind, ask the person if they would like to share it with you. You don't need a lot of detail, just enough to know where you are in the process, and what to pray next. Usually, the first thing that comes into their mind is the next thing to bring to God.

God speaks to people in a variety of ways. He may bring a thought, a feeling, a memory or a Scripture to their mind. He may remind them of a song, show them a picture, bring peace, lift burdens, or speak in other ways. Memories that God brings to mind may be ones the person often thinks about. Or they may be experiences that have been forgotten or even dissociated.

When we pray with someone, we're always learning how they interact with God, and how they interact with us. Some people prefer to share substantially. Others may say very little. If they are silent for a long time they might be in deep communion with God throughout. Or they might be stuck in the process. If someone seems stuck in a negative emotion for longer than a minute or two, you may want to pray verses of comfort and truth. Ask God for wisdom on this.

Keep in mind the main principle of Wholeness Prayer: *Follow Jesus.*
- Don't push the person to work through issues. If they seem hesitant to pursue any part of the Wholeness Prayer process, ask them how they're feeling about continuing the process. If they want to work through any negative thoughts and/or feelings about continuing with the process, then help them to take these

thoughts and/or feelings captive and follow the 5 R's. If they have negative thoughts and/or feelings about pursuing the process, but aren't ready to work through them, that's okay. Pray a closing prayer of blessing and protection over them, if they are willing for you to do so. God can meet them in His way and time.
- Pray open-ended prayers. *Don't* suggest what God might be saying or doing in a memory. You may, at times, want to ask God to reveal if there are specific emotions present (e.g. fear, hurt, shame or frustration underlying anger) or specific issues to address (forgiveness, trauma, grief, vows). If you do, accept the person's answer. Don't push them to give the answer you expect.

If a negative emotion is triggered within you as you pray for others, pray through this afterward. If you'd like assistance, ask someone to help you.

Consistency in the following areas is very important:
- Practice compassionate detachment. Care but don't carry the problem(s).
- Show respect for the person being prayed for. They are precious to God, not a project or something to "fix."
- Maintain humility. Give all the glory to God.
- Keep confidentiality. Don't share other people's stories without prior permission.

If any of these is hard for you, there may be related root issues for you to pray through.

Generally, it's best if men pray with men, and women pray with women. If you're praying with someone of the opposite gender, or in any situation where there might be sexual attraction between you, have someone else either join you or be close enough to see you at all times. Do not pray with anyone in a place that could provide an opportunity for impropriety, or even the appearance of impropriety.

Stopping in the middle of the process. Sometimes you need to end a Wholeness Prayer time before God's peace fully enters a memory or pattern. When this happens, ask God to bless the person being prayed for, protect every unhealed place in them and bring healing soon. Thank Him for what He has already done. Then pray a closing prayer (page 12).

Resuming praying through an ongoing issue. When resuming the process of praying through an ongoing issue, first pray an opening prayer. Then ask God to reveal, to the person being prayed for, where they are in the process and what would be good to pray through next. Thank Him for what He has already done, then continue the prayer time.

Not needing all the details. The person being prayed for doesn't need to tell the one praying for them all about the issue or everything that is happening as they process. It's enough to share the big picture – so that the person praying for them knows where they are in the process and what they might want to pray next.

Struggling with the same or similar thoughts or feelings. Sometimes the person who was prayed for and experienced a breakthrough later struggles with the same thoughts or feelings. Or they may find it difficult to consistently apply the truths God has revealed through Wholeness Prayer. If this happens, they may conclude that nothing has changed. In reality, a change has happened, but something has overwhelmed their capacity to walk in the new truth. If the person is willing, use Wholeness Prayer principles to bring the struggle to God and ask Him to show the way forward. It may be that there are more issues to process. Or it might be that the new path that Jesus has revealed is not yet a habit. After the Wholeness Prayer process is used to pray through a specific feeling or belief, the person who was prayed for sometimes later experiences a feeling or thought *similar* to the one which was addressed. If this happens, there may be a related false belief that has yet to be addressed. Follow the Wholeness Prayer process to pray through the feeling or belief.

If you pray with someone multiple times and they experience breakthroughs, but later can't remember or apply these, they may have a pattern of being robbed of their victories. If they are willing, help them to take this pattern captive and pray through it using Wholeness Prayer.

2-way conversation. If you are a follower of Christ, you may want to work through some issues without a third party facilitating. Before doing so, we recommend you
- understand basic Wholeness Prayer principles
- pray through Freedom from Generational Bondage (page 53) and Freedom from Occult Bondage (page 59)
- pray through any major issues such as traumas.

If you use Wholeness Prayer principles to start praying through something on your own and then get stuck, stop and ask another believer for help. Also ask for help if you find yourself experiencing overwhelming emotions or you feel spiritually attacked. Ask for help, too, if you have reason to suspect that serious spiritual warfare may be part of the issue you're about to address, or if for any other reason you begin to feel you would prefer working through these things with someone else.

Wholeness Prayer Team. The more difficult the issues being prayed through, the greater the need for a larger prayer team. The need also increases for individual and group prayer and fasting. This can be done before, during and after the prayer times.

Following is a sample Wholeness Prayer team for a more complex issue.

Function	Definition and Explanation of Role	Gifts and Characteristics Needed
Pray-ee	*The person receiving prayer ministry:* This person is being empowered to hear biblical truth directly from God at their place of need.	Awareness of need

Desire for change

Willingness to be prayed for in this way |
| Pray-er | *The person facilitating the prayer time:* This person is partnering with God to facilitate the pray-ee hearing directly from Him at their point of need. (This is very different from praying *for* or *over* the person.) | Ability to facilitate the process *(including a working knowledge of Wholeness Prayer)*

Good listening skills
Sufficient faith, hope, love and wisdom

Ability to communicate sincere affirmation

Basic knowledge of biblical truth

Ability to discern truth |
| Prophetic Seer | *This person may receive pictures (or other information) from God that reveal the point of need (or other things important to the process).* | Ability to keep quiet unless called on (This person is encouraged to communicate with the pray-er by writing notes, or whispering when appropriate.) *The more difficult the issue, the more need for this function to be done by a separate person.* |

Knowledge of biblical Truth	This person may help to identify Scriptures that speak to the point of need. They may also be used by God to teach biblical truth as needed to complement the Wholeness Prayer process.	Same as Prophetic Seer.
Discernment of Spirits	This person may receive information from God about the spiritual dynamics involved.	Same as Prophetic Seer.
Backup Pray-er	This person may or may not be present. They may pray at the exact time of ministry and/or at other times.	Same as Prophetic Seer.

During a Wholeness Prayer time, the prayer team may find it helpful to take periodic breaks to communicate with one another about the situation at hand. Afterward, a time of debriefing together as a team may be helpful in assessing progress and stuck places. At that time, the team can also address anything triggered in team members that needs to be prayed through, and identify things to potentially do or not do in similar situations.

A good prayer team will include high levels of spiritual maturity, holiness, compassionate detachment, patience, and willingness to let the Holy Spirit guide the process. More difficult issues also call for an increased ability to respond with grace and love (not judgment) and a working knowledge of one's authority in Christ over the evil one. It's essential that everyone on the ministry team keeps confidentiality and does not share other people's stories without prior permission.

The prayer team may meet multiple times with the person being prayed for. The more complex the issue, the more important is the role of a broader healthy relational community (beyond the prayer team) for ongoing healing.

If you notice signs of spiritual interference[8] **during the ministry time**, ask God again to protect you. Bind and rebuke any interference. Ask God to show you the reason for the interference. Follow Him to address any strongholds, unconfessed sin, occult issues, or anything else that might give the evil one a foothold. Command any demonic elements (that previously had a foothold because of something that's now been taken care of) to go now where Jesus sends them and never return.

If you still notice interference, close the ministry time with prayer, then seek counsel from trusted advisors while keeping confidentiality. Strong spiritual opposition may best be addressed by a ministry team. "Again, truly I tell you that if two of you on earth agree about anything they ask for, it will be done for them by my Father in heaven. For where two or three gather in my name, there am I with them" (Matthew 18:19-20, NIV).

If you have any doubt of your authority in Christ, work through this issue. Use Wholeness Prayer as needed to process this and any other issues that emerge.

After praying for someone else, ask God (together with another mature follower of Christ, or with your ministry team) to cleanse you from anything that is not of Him. Give God any burdens you may be carrying on behalf of the person. Ask God to fill you with Himself and with joy. Give God the glory. Thank and praise Him! As soon as possible, pray through any negative thoughts or emotions that were triggered in you during the prayer time.

Know when to refer. If you (or your team) are praying with someone and issues arise that are more advanced than you feel equipped to deal with, seek an alternate route. It may be best to ask the person with whom you've been praying whether you can refer them to someone else. While nothing is too advanced for God, someone else may be more equipped than we are to help with some issues.

Chapter 5. Hindrances to Wholeness Prayer

Along the journey toward wholeness, there may be hindrances related to hearing God, connecting with feelings, and more. This chapter discusses some common hindrances, many of which need to be addressed before continuing with the basic Wholeness Prayer process. While some hindrances can affect more than one part of the process, the overall flow of this chapter begins with general hindrances, then considers those that may affect each of the 5 R's (Recognize, Recent, Root, Receive, and Renew).

General hindrances
- Sometimes issues emerge that need teaching, counseling, or intercession rather than Wholeness Prayer. If this is the case, help the person to pursue what is needed.
- There may be cultural or positional barriers to people sharing openly with one another. For example, a leader may feel they have to preserve an image of not having any issues.[9]
- The person may have sin that they've not yet confessed and turned from (page 99), some type of occult bondage that's not yet been dealt with (page 59), or someone they've not yet forgiven (page 101).
- There may be spiritual interference (page 42). If this is still the case after praying an opening prayer, ask God to reveal why.
- The person may be feeling confused. If so, it may help to share 1 Corinthians 14:33b with them, "God is not a God of confusion but of peace…."[10] Then rebuke any confusion in Jesus' name and ask God to bring His peace.
- There may be a sense of spiritual darkness. In this case, rebuke the darkness and ask God to bring His light and truth.
- The person may have repressed or dissociated[11] feelings, beliefs or memories. This could be an effect of trauma (page 83) or other issues.
- The person may need to grow in foundational joy (page 191) and security before pursuing deeper issues. The pain involved in

accessing their memories may be more than they can currently process.
- The person may be overtired and need to rest.
- There may be issues in *your* life that are interfering with the process. For example, you might be afraid you won't facilitate the process correctly, or the issue that came up might have triggered an issue in your own life. If this happens, work through these issues after concluding the prayer time. If you'd like help, ask someone to help you.

When you're not sure how to proceed, ask God for direction. This is part of the main Wholeness Prayer principle: *Follow Jesus.* While the facilitator will consistently be silently asking God how to proceed, there are times when it may be helpful to ask God for direction as a group. We might ask, "God, would You please show us how to proceed?" Then wait in silence for a bit. He may speak to anyone present.

If the person is having trouble hearing God, ask Him to reveal why.

God may be speaking to them in ways they've not yet learned to recognize. He might bring thoughts or memories to mind, or give new insight into an issue. He could speak through Scripture, through nature, dreams, music or pictures, or audibly. Or He may communicate with them in some other way.

They may have theological reservations about God speaking to His people. Or they may lack good biblical teaching about who God is, or lack good biblical teaching in general.

They may feel that asking God to speak to them is unrealistic or unwise for some reason. For example, they might find it hard to trust God fully, or be afraid that asking God to speak to them could lead to disappointment or punishment. They may feel that God is distant, uncaring, or harsh. If this is the case, ask God to reveal why they feel that way and work through the issues that emerge. Possible reasons include
- They feel similarly about someone who has had great influence on their life – for example, one of their parents. In this case, they may be assuming that God's character has similar

weaknesses to those they've seen in that person's character (page 79).
- They may have emotional wounds that need to be healed (page 67) or internal strongholds that need to be broken (page 129).
- They may have anger (page 72), unconfessed sin (page 99), unforgiveness (page 101), or other issues that need to be addressed first.

There may be a reason why the person doesn't want to have something revealed. Perhaps they want to avoid facing what happened, how they felt, what they believed, the root of the issue, or God's perspective. If this might be the case, ask God to show them if there's any reason why they wouldn't *want* to know. Then work through any issues that emerge.

Occasionally the person being prayed for repeatedly talks to God more than listening to Him. As a result, they may have a hard time hearing Him. Sometimes, after you pray and ask God to reveal something, the person being prayed for repeatedly prays aloud as well (instead of listening to God and receiving from Him). If this happens, they may not yet understand how the Wholeness Prayer process generally works. If the person is having a hard time connecting with God, it may help to ask them to let you do the verbal praying. Encourage them to focus on listening to God and receiving from Him, then sharing as much (or little) of that with you as they desire.

Sometimes a person struggles to hear God in the present, although they have heard Him speak in the past. In such cases, it sometimes helps to
- Ask God to remind the person of the last time He spoke to them. Then ask God to show the person what happened after that. Work through any issues that emerge.
- Ask God to show the person if there's something He'd like to talk about with them. Then spend time listening quietly.
- Encourage the person to invite God in and ask Him to help them hear Him.
- Encourage the person to thank God for at least five things (e.g. loved one, nature, recent event, answered prayer, daily

blessings). Then ask God to show them if there are ways He would like to connect with them (or already has connected with them) through these blessings.
- More ideas can be found in Growing in Hearing God <http://ent.freemin.org/hearing-god/>.

If what emerges in the person's mind is something or someone outside themselves. After asking God to help the person recognize what *within them* would be good to pray through at this time, sometimes they instead desire to pray for someone else or a broader situation. In such a case
- Bring this desire to God. Ask Him to show the person being prayed for anything within them that would be good to pray through first. For example, how they feel or what they believe about the issue.
- Use Wholeness Prayer to pray through the underlying issues that emerge.
- Intercede together for the initial prayer burden.

If nothing is revealed. If nothing is revealed after asking God to reveal a belief, feeling or memory, ask God to reveal why nothing emerged. Then ask the person what they're thinking and feeling, especially the *first thing* that came to mind.

Sometimes something did come to the person's mind, but they're not recognizing it as significant. They may be discounting what came to mind, thinking that it's not important. In this case, it can help to tell them that usually the first thing that comes to mind is the one to pursue.

People may have negative thoughts or emotions related to nothing being revealed. If they do, it's possible that those thoughts or emotions are acting as a block against healing. For example, they may feel discouraged or hopeless, or struggle with doubt. Behind those feelings may be a belief such as "Even though this process has worked for others, it won't help me," or "I'll never change." If the person has a feeling or belief blocking further healing, start by addressing that.

If the person has trouble connecting with their feelings or no feelings are revealed. Sometimes a memory, thought or action has been recognized as needing Wholeness Prayer, but no corresponding feelings have yet been identified. In such a case, ask God to reveal any underlying *emotions* related to the thoughts or actions that have already been revealed.
Some people are disconnected from their emotions, or don't want to connect with some or all of them for some reason. In such cases, it may be helpful to work through Connecting with Feelings <http://ent.freemin.org/connecting-with-feelings/>.

If a person's feelings have been revealed, but they are having trouble connecting with these in a memory, ask God to show them if there's any reason why they wouldn't *want* to connect with their feelings. If no reason comes to mind, ask them if they'd be willing to feel, for a short time, as much of this feeling as is needed to facilitate the healing process. If they are willing, encourage them to ask God to help them do this. (Choosing that they *really* want to connect with these feelings can help to address this hindrance.)

If there is a reason they don't want to connect with their feelings, this is the next thing to work through. For example, they may have a fear of emotional pain. If this is the case, ask them if they'd be willing to take their fear of emotional pain captive and pray through it.

If the person being prayed for starts to analyze more than connect with their feeling and beliefs, they may get stuck. If so, you might want to see if they're willing to connect with their feelings and beliefs, and bring those to Jesus. If so, it may help to ask God to help them to do this now. If they aren't willing to connect with their feelings, it may help to ask God to show them why, then work through any issues that emerge.

On the other hand, the person may seem to be analyzing, when Jesus is actually already revealing to them (using whatever ways He speaks to them) how various things have been interrelated in their life. This can be a very powerful part of the process. The key factor is determining what Jesus is doing, and following Him.

Some people connect more with their thoughts than their feelings. If the Wholeness Prayer process is moving forward, and the person is receiving truth and being renewed, keep following Jesus through the Wholeness Prayer process and giving Him praise. If the person becomes stuck at some point in the process, it might be good to ask God to reveal if any feelings are being repressed or denied.

If no false beliefs are revealed. If it is difficult for the person receiving ministry to identify any false beliefs, it may help to ask them if they know what they were thinking and feeling during the memory. If they do, then ask them to share with you as much as they want to of any thoughts and feelings from the memory. Sometimes it's easier for you to recognize the false beliefs, since you are less likely to believe them.

If the person being prayed for continues to have trouble identifying or clarifying the false beliefs, ask Jesus why. It may be that the original or key memory has not yet been revealed. Or there could be internal strongholds in the person's life that need to be addressed first (page 129).

In some cases, there are no false beliefs in the memory. There may still be unpleasant emotions based on truth (page 71), or other issues to work through, together with God.

If no root memory or pattern emerges. If no root memory or pattern is revealed, ask God to reveal why. Then ask the person being prayed for what they're thinking or feeling.

Sometimes God will first bring to mind memories which are not the original memory or a key memory in a pattern, but which include helpful information for further identifying related feelings, false beliefs or other issues. In this case, continue to bring to God the things that come to the person's mind. As they think and feel as much as God wants them to, of the thoughts and feelings they had in the revealed memory, ask God to reveal the root or key memory. Continue to do this until the root or key memory is revealed. In most cases this will be a childhood memory.

People have different kinds of memories. Emotional memories are the most common. Memories can also involve any of the five senses:

smell, hearing, taste, sight, and touch. The body may also react with muscle tension, headache, nausea or cramping, breathing difficulty, inner aches and pains, or other physical sensations.

If an emotional memory or pattern doesn't come into the person's mind, ask God to help them be aware of anything they're experiencing physically, or through their other senses. For example, they might feel pressure on their chest, or a knot in their stomach. In this case, ask God to help them feel this as much as He wants them to, for a moment in His presence. Then ask Him to show them the first time (page 10) they felt this way (or if it's a pattern or generational)[12].

If no root or key memory is revealed, there may be a false belief guarding the memory. If you think this might be the case, you can ask God to show the person being prayed for if there's any reason why they wouldn't *want* to access the memory. If there is, pray through that issue first.

It's possible that the person being prayed for may have learned to respond in a certain way because this is what their parents (or another significant person in their life) modeled. For example, a woman may have learned to disrespect men because her mother did. If this is the case, ask God to bring to the person's mind the first (or key) memory (or pattern) where they saw someone else acting in this way. (This may be where they learned this way to act, feel, think or respond.)

If no truth is revealed in the root memory or pattern (when false beliefs are involved). Sometimes the person being prayed for doesn't receive truth in the memory after you've asked God to reveal it to them. If this happens, ask them if *they* would like to invite Jesus to come into the memory and reveal His truth. This step is especially helpful when someone has been abused.

It's possible that the person may be receiving truth, but not recognizing it as such. People hear from God in different ways. Words of truth may come to their mind, they may be reminded of a Scripture, see a picture (of something in the memory, for example), hear a song, or simply realize the truth. Or God may reveal truth to them in another way. Receiving truth brings release from the pain of the false belief.

If truth has not yet been revealed in the memory, ask Jesus why. Some possibilities include
- You haven't yet found the original or key memory.
- The person needs to forgive themselves (page 113).
- There are internal strongholds in the person's life that need to be addressed first (page 129).

If the "truth" revealed is false. Sometimes the "truth" people think they are receiving is not consistent with Scripture. Anything contrary to the Bible is not truth. If something false is being revealed, treat it as a false belief. Ask God to help the person think or feel as much of it as He wants them to now, and, as they do, to show them the first time they felt or believed this way, or if it has been a pattern in their life. Continue to work through the false belief until God's truth is revealed. If the person has received false teaching, they may also need to be taught biblical truth.

In some cases, a false Jesus may appear in the memory. The appearance of a false Jesus often indicates a conflict the person has about how they see God, themselves, or others. Instead of revealing truth, a false Jesus will speak unloving words or behave in an ungodly way. It cannot represent goodness for very long. If a false Jesus appears in a memory, rebuke it in the name of the *True* Lord Jesus Christ of Nazareth. Ask the True Jesus to reveal what this conflict is and where it began. Then seek God's truth at the root.

If the root memory is not yet peaceful, continue to pray through issues that emerge until there is peace throughout the memory.

If the *person* does not yet feel peaceful, continue to pray through issues that emerge until they feel peaceful. There may be more than one issue or memory to process.

If it's time for the prayer session to end before you finish working through the issues, see the previous chapter for ideas on stopping in the middle of the process and continuing another time (page 38).

Part 2. Keys for Nine Common Issues

These keys are designed to be used together with the basic Wholeness Prayer principles and 5 R's introduced in Part 1. They give concrete ideas for filling in this general framework.

In general, we find it most helpful to first pray through generational bondage (page 53) and any occult bondage (page 59), before seeking to address other issues within the person.

Chapter 6. Freedom from Generational Bondage[13]

The Lord, the Lord, the compassionate and gracious God,
slow to anger, abounding in love and faithfulness,
maintaining love to thousands,
and forgiving wickedness, rebellion and sin.
Yet he does not leave the guilty unpunished;
he punishes the children and their children
for the sin of the parents to the third and fourth generation.
~Exodus 34:6b-7 (NIV)

It is for freedom that Christ has set us free. Stand firm, then,
and do not let yourselves be burdened again by a yoke of slavery.
~Galatians 5:1 (NIV)

Lois, a long-time intercessor with a great love for people, had longed to hear God for decades. We had lifted this up to God in multiple Wholeness Prayer sessions, but her struggle remained. After she prayed through freedom from generational bondage (page 53), she began to hear God clearly. Since that time she's grown in intimacy with God, and in confidence of His love for her.

Every person is affected positively and negatively by the members of their family. We learn by watching and imitating those around us. For example, if verbal arguments occurred daily in one's family of origin, this pattern often becomes accepted as a normal way to interact with others.

If a trend or pattern shows itself over several generations, there is the possibility that generational sin is present in the family line. Generational sin is like any other sin. It needs to be dealt with by confessing the sin to God and repenting of the behavior.

Identifying and confessing unhealthy and sinful generational patterns can help people get free from sin, negative traits and unhealthy patterns similar to those of their ancestors. In addition, they will also need to address patterns in their lives that have taken root as a result of their own choices and experiences. For example, if there has been a pattern of lying in a person's family of origin, first ask God to free them from any generational bondage related to this. They will also benefit from working through any underlying reasons why they have personally chosen to lie.

Most people will benefit from praying through freedom from generational bondage. Doing this often brings increased peace and greater ability to pray through and overcome root issues. Sometimes the effects of praying through freedom from generational bondage are dramatic.

When praying with a follower of Christ who desires freedom from generational bondage, we find the following steps helpful:

- Begin with an opening prayer (page 8). As part of this prayer, ask God to help the person identify any areas of generational bondage that they need to be aware of.
- Ask the person to prayerfully look over the chart on the following two pages, and speak out anything they know of in their own lives or feel might possibly be generational.
- Ask God to show them if there are other areas to include, either on the list or not on the list.
- After the areas of generational bondage are identified, ask the person to read silently through the sample prayer. Then have them decide what they would like to pray (whether or not it includes part or all of the sample prayer).
- Invite the person to pray aloud, while you agree with them in prayer.
- After the person prays as they feel led, ask God to reveal if there are any additional things for the person to do or pray in follow-up. This may include repenting of sins in which they themselves have participated (page 99), getting free from the effects of occult involvement (page 59), and praying through root issues that emerge.
- At the end of the prayer time, pray a closing prayer (page 12).

Potential Generational Sins, Negative Patterns or Inherited Traits[14]

Sexual Issues	Addictions	Physical / Psychological
fornication	alcohol	physical problems
adultery	tobacco	infertility
perversions	drugs	depression
pornography	gambling	insanity
incest	food	psychological issues
conceived out of wedlock	obsessive / compulsive	
lust	workaholism	

Death	Marriage Issues	Abuse
miscarriages	unhealthy relational dynamics	physical
abortions		emotional
still birth		spiritual
early death		sexual
accidental death	divorce	abusive relationships
suicide		
murder		

Religious / Idolatrous		
ancestor worship	witchcraft	eastern religions
syncretism	traditional ceremonies	curses
occult practices		rebellion
psychic practices	traditional healers	love of money / power
worship of false gods	following false religions	prejudice
spirit worship		fear of man
idol worship	religious cults	unbelief

Unhealthy emotions	Personal / Relational	Blame / Self-Punishment
anger/rage	lying	self-blame
unforgiveness	selfishness	self-accusation
bitterness	laziness	self-hatred
shame	gossip / slander	self-destruction
guilt	negativity	self-criticism
pride	manipulating	self-shame
fear	others	self-anger
worry/anxiety	unhealthy	
insecurity	control	
perfectionism	deception	
hopelessness	criticism	
fear of rejection	blame shifting	
fear of abandonment	revenge	
	avoiding	
hatred of men	responsibility	
hatred of women	fear of intimacy / commitment	
envy		
worthlessness		
apathy		

Sample Prayer[15]

I confess the sins, negative patterns and traits of my ancestors that I've identified. I specifically include the following: (List issues as you feel led.)

I renounce, reject and disown all the sins, negative patterns and traits of my ancestors. I repent of their beliefs, their actions and their unrighteous behavior. I declare the assignments, the curses and the powers flowing from those curses to be null and void. I break all rights, grounds, or privileges that these sins have had in my life and I will live under their authority no longer, because I belong to Jesus Christ.

I place the cross of Jesus Christ between me and anything I need protection from regarding each member of my family (Name any ancestors you desire.) and all those I have not known or named. I reject any and every way that Satan claims ownership over me. By the authority that I have in Jesus Christ, I now command every familial and ancestral spirit to be bound in chains and be stripped of all armor, weapons, power, authority and illusions. I command that they now throw down at the foot of the cross of Jesus Christ all plans, programs, agendas and assignments that they have had in my life. I command that they now return everything that they have stolen from me emotionally, mentally, physically and spiritually. I command that they go to the place Jesus sends them.

Jesus, I invite You to fill me now with Your Holy Spirit. I ask You to build a spiritual wall of protection between me and anything I need protection from regarding my mother, and between me and anything I need protection from regarding my father and all their ancestors. Make these protective walls as high and wide as they need to be, to provide complete spiritual protection, and seal those walls with the blood of Christ. At the same time, please bless my relationship with each member of my family who is still living and help us to grow in good and healthy ways together.

I come before You now God, as Your child, purchased by the blood of Christ. Let the blood of Christ completely cleanse my own bloodline. I commit myself to the renewing of my mind, and I align my will with Your good and perfect will. All this I do in the name and authority of the Lord Jesus Christ. Amen.

Keys
- Identify generational bondage at work in their family of origin.
- They confess this and ask God to protect them.
- Work through any follow-up steps.

Chapter 7. Freedom from Occult Bondage

*Do not worship any other god,
for the LORD, whose name is Jealous, is a jealous God.*
~Exodus 34:14 (NIV)

*The reason the Son of God appeared
was to destroy the devil's work.*
~1 John 3:8b (NIV)

> "Susi focuses on mobilizing others in Indonesia to minister to unreached people groups. She received a massage from a local masseuse. After that she became unable to pray for the unreached and lost all desire to read her Bible. Without her knowledge, the masseuse had incorporated occult practices into the massage. Through Wholeness Prayer God freed her to again read the Scripture and mobilize others to minister among the unreached." ~L, Indonesia

When Theresa was a new believer, she avoided spending time with God. She often fell asleep or heard disturbing voices when she read the Bible. She prayed with Joyce through Freedom from Generational Bondage and renounced the sins of her ancestors, including the sin of witchcraft. After that she was able to read the Bible without interference. Her intimacy with God has grown exponentially since then.

When you're facilitating a time of Wholeness Prayer, occult bondage may emerge as an issue to address. Until it's addressed, it can affect the person being prayed for in many ways, including hindering the person's ability to hear God, engage with the Wholeness Prayer process, and experience breakthroughs.

"The word 'occult' is generally associated with secret knowledge and practices dealing with the supernatural or 'psychic' phenomena, often for the purpose of obtaining personal power. Some occult practices rely on demons or 'spirits' to achieve their goals."[16]

Occult bondage can result from a wide range of activities. These include, but are not limited to: astrology, spirit-guided writing, calling up spirits of dead people, demon worship, divination, enchantments, fortune telling, Freemasonry, horoscopes, mediums, Ouija boards, palm reading, Satanism, sorcery, spirit guides, Tarot cards, voodoo, Wicca and witchcraft.[17]

If someone's family of origin has engaged in occult practices, they may be suffering from occult bondage even if they themselves have not knowingly been involved in any occult activity. Their family's past or present involvement may increase their own desire to pursue occult practices, as may their own hurts and struggles.

When someone confesses their occult involvement, renounces it, and asks God to forgive them and break its effects in their life, rights are taken away from evil spirits who have gained influence over them.[18] The person also needs to follow through with any action steps that God reveals, such as destroying objects of power. And they need to present their bodies as living sacrifices to God (Romans 12:1) and rely only on Him for protection.

If you've been involved in the occult and have now given your life to Christ, we recommend you ask for on-site help from mature followers of Christ when praying through these issues.

When you're helping someone to pray through occult bondage, we recommend that another follower of Christ who is reasonably mature also be present and backing you up in prayer. If neither of you has much experience in helping others pray through occult bondage, it may be best to refer them to someone else (page 42).

When praying with a follower of Christ who's seeking freedom from occult bondage, you may find these steps helpful:
- Ask God to reveal to the person all ways in which they have been involved in the occult (page 66). If there are any,
  - Ask God to reveal anything within them that contributed to their decision to be involved in the occult.

- o Work through any related issues, such as confessing and turning from sin (page 99), healing from emotional wounds (page 67), forgiveness (page 101), and breaking internal strongholds (page 129) such as judging (page 139) or cursing others (page 134).
- o Ask the person to pray as they feel led through Sample Prayer for Occult Involvement (page 63) and Sample Prayer for Confession of Idolatrous Worship (page 64).
- Ask God to reveal, to the person being prayed for, all ways in which others have been involved in the occult on their behalf, whether they were seeking "good" or harm. If there are any such ways,
  - o Ask the person to pray as they feel led through Sample Prayer for Occult Oppression (page 66), adapting it to their situation.
  - o Work through any related issues, such as forgiveness (page 101), healing for emotional wounds (page 67), and breaking internal strongholds (page 129) including curses (page 135).
- Ask God to break the power of occult bondage in the person's life, shut every door to evil in the person's life, fill every part of the person with Christ, and protect the person and their family.
- Ask God to remind the person being prayed for of any occult objects of theirs that haven't yet been destroyed.
  - o If the person has any occult objects, ask God to show them any issues to address before destroying these. Pray through any issues that emerge, and help them find answers to any questions they have.
  - o Together with them and at least one other spiritually mature follower of Christ, appropriately destroy all occult objects they possess.
    - Pray together over the object to totally break its power.
    - Ask God to totally break any power the object has had over them.
    - Burn or break the object beyond recognition and usefulness.
    - Dispose of it in a place where no one will be tempted to retrieve it.
- Ask God to show the person any other follow-up steps to pursue.

Keys
- Identify, confess and repent of occult involvement.
- Pray through related issues.
- Break the power of occult bondage in the person's life.
- Ask God to shut every door to evil in the person's life.
- Ask God to fill every part of the person with Christ.
- Destroy occult objects.
- Ask God to protect the person and their family.

Incomplete List of Occult Practices

Astrology	Fortune-telling	Reincarnation
Automatic Writing	Handwriting Analysis	Satanic Ritual Abuse
Black Arts		
Black Magic	Horoscopes	Satanism
Black Mass	I Ching	Séances
Chakras	Idol Worship	Sorcery
Channeling	Incantations	Superstition
Charlie-Charlie	Incubus/Succubus	Table-Tipping
Charms	Demon	Talismans
Clairaudience	Levitation	Tarot Cards
Clairvoyance	Mediums	Telepathy
Contacting the Dead	Ouija boards	Transcendental Mediation
	Pendulum Healing	
Devil's Pentagram	Phrenology	White Magic
Divination	Person Programming	Wicca
Eastern Star	Psychic Healing	Witchcraft
Extrasensory Perception	Psychic Portrait	Voodoo
	Psychics	Yoga
Fetishes	Pyramid ology	Zodiac Studies
Free Masonry	Reading Tea Leaves	

Sample Prayer for Occult Involvement (for a follower of Christ)[19] – to use whichever portions are relevant to their situation.

Lord God, I repent of my participation in the occult. Forgive me for any practices by which I knowingly or unknowingly invited the involvement of evil spirits in my life.

I sought help through the occult in these ways: [State type of involvement.] Please forgive and cleanse me. Save me from the consequences of my sin. I confess that any spirits that came to me which I thought were for my benefit, are really evil spirits who want to destroy me.

In the name of Jesus, I reject all benefits, abilities, blessings or powers: [Speak out anything that comes to mind.] obtained through occult encounters. In the name of Jesus, I rescind any occult pacts or covenants I made: [Speak out any agreements made.] I am under the new covenant established by the blood of Jesus Christ. In Jesus' name I renounce the taking in of any occult substance – food, drink or potions. I receive the forgiveness and cleansing of Jesus.

Together with those who are here supporting me in prayer, I command all items inserted by magical power to come out now in Jesus' name. We bring to You, Lord God, any items connected to the occult. We break their power in the name of Jesus. Please give me strength to destroy charms, amulets or any other object that is associated with dark powers. [These should be destroyed as soon as possible. See When praying with a follower of Christ who's seeking freedom from occult bondage (page 60).]

In the name of Jesus, we command all evil spirits connected with this occult involvement to go immediately to the place where Jesus sends you. We forbid you to touch me, my family, or any of my descendants. Lord God, I receive from You alone all help, blessings, healing, abilities, power, gifts or protection that You want to give me, to replace what the enemy had given me. Please show me any inner wounds that may have influenced me to turn to the occult and please help me to seek and find healing for those. I choose to live for You alone. Please fill me with Your love and protect me by Your power. In Jesus' mighty name, Amen.

Sample Prayer for Confession of Idolatrous Worship (for a follower of Christ)[20]

I proclaim my faith in Jesus Christ, as my Lord and Savior.

Lord God, I come before Your presence to acknowledge that I sinned against You when I knowingly and unknowingly turned from You by not following Your greatest commandment, "Love the Lord your God with all your heart and with all your soul and with all your mind."[21]

In rebellion and ignorance I chose to follow false teachers, and I have participated in occult practices and idolatrous worship. Have mercy on me, God!

I recognize that there is only one true and living God (Isaiah 45:22), who exists as the Father, Son (Jesus Christ of Nazareth) and Holy Spirit. I acknowledge that You are the only omniscient (all-knowing), omnipotent (all-powerful) and omnipresent (always and everywhere present) God.

I also acknowledge that the resurrected Lord Jesus Christ has been given all authority in Heaven and on earth and that He has supremacy in everything (Colossians 1:15-18).

I have invited Jesus Christ into my life as my Lord and Savior and I believe that I am now a child of God (1 John 3:1-3). I believe that by faith and the grace of God, I am seated with Christ in the heavenly realms (Ephesians 2:6); and that when I was still a sinner, Christ died for me (Romans 5:8). I believe that Jesus has delivered me from the domain of darkness and transferred me to His Kingdom and that in Him I have redemption, the forgiveness of sins (Colossians 1:13-14).

Lord God, I acknowledge that You are the God of truth. I have been deceived by the father of lies (John 8:44) and I have deceived myself. I pray that, with the help of Your Holy Spirit, You lead me into all truth and reveal to me now all the ways that I have turned from You and either knowingly or unknowingly participated in or been involved in false religions, cultic or occult practices, or worshipped and followed false teachers and false gods.

[For each occult activity being confessed, pray:] *Lord God, I acknowledge, confess and take full responsibility for sinning against You when I participated in _____. I renounce my participation in and involvement with _____ and I commit myself to the Lord Jesus Christ, who is the way and the truth and the life (John 14:6).*

I bind my sin of idolatry to the cross of Jesus Christ. Lord God, I humble myself and ask for Your forgiveness for all my unholy thoughts and activities. I now receive Your forgiveness. Please purify me from my unrighteousness. Set me free by Your grace and mercy.

Lord God, I turn to You now and repent of my sin of idolatry. Remove from me any further desire to separate myself from You. I commit to worshipping only You, the one true God – the Creator, the Sustainer, the Protector, the True God of Love and Life.

Lord God, I ask You now to break any rights, grounds or privileges that I gained in my life as a result of this inappropriate spiritual worship. Amen.

[After addressing all occult practices, using a prayer such as the one above, pray:]
Lord God, thank You for releasing me from the bondage of my unbelief. Thank You that You are all I need. I choose obedience to You alone and I place my confidence in You. Protect me, Lord God, from any counterattack from the world of darkness and help me to live in the freedom of the cross. Thank You that You have disarmed the enemy and that Jesus Christ has already won the victory. I claim that victory in my life.

Thank You that I am, by faith, a child of God. I am purchased by the blood of Jesus, redeemed, free of condemnation, accepted and a friend of Christ. Thank You for forgiving me and setting me free. In the wonderful name of the Lord Jesus Christ, Amen.

Sample Prayer for Occult Oppression (for a follower of Christ)[22]

Oh God, I believe that others have used magical powers to try to help me. Help me to forgive [name of person] for what they did [State type of involvement.] in order to obtain something on my behalf. [State type of help being sought.]

In the name of Jesus, I reject any help, benefit, blessing, healing, protection, ability or power supplied by evil spirits. In Jesus' name, I renounce the taking in of any occult substance – food, drink or potions. I trust in the sacrifice and blood of Jesus Christ which is stronger than anything else.

Together with those who are here supporting me in prayer, in the name of Jesus, we break the power of any mantras or spells that were said on my behalf. In the name of Jesus, we break the power of any pacts or vows made on my behalf. In the name of Jesus, we order out any evil spirits who may have come to me as a result of someone else's involvement in the occult.

Lord Jesus, I receive from You all help, blessings, healing, abilities, power, gifts and protection that You want to give me, to replace what the enemy gave. Thank You for coming to destroy the works of the devil, and giving me abundant life. Please show me any hurts connected with this occult oppression and help me to seek and find healing for those. I open my heart to You. In Jesus' mighty name, Amen.

Chapter 8. Healing from Emotional Wounds

*I pray that you, being rooted and established in love, may have power, together with all the Lord's holy people, to grasp how wide and long and high and deep is the love of Christ,
and to know this love that surpasses knowledge—
that you may be filled to the measure of all the fullness of God.*
~Ephesians 3:17b-19 (NIV)

"My time with Jean was encouraging, insightful, and helpful as we prayed over Skype through thoughts and patterns of sin that the Lord brought to mind. In many cases I remember being shown how the evil one had been working to establish a lie which I believed as truth. I feel this was a root cause for feeling distant from God and unworthy to serve Him in any meaningful way. An example of this was seeing an image of the enemy accusing me and throwing dirty clothes on me. Then the Lord rebuked him. After that, He brought to mind all the different truths of my sonship found in Him and why I am clean.

I felt the picture was confirmed, as being from the Lord, when a brother showed me (unknowing of my experience) a passage in Zechariah 3:1-5 where clean and new garments were put onto the priest Joshua. In the past I could have explained the theological reasons that I was clean before the Lord and how I am a new creature in Him. But I had one little place in my heart where I held onto a lie that I would never be clean enough, never measure up, and always be burdened with sin.

The outcome of what we touched on was always positive with there being immediate results in some cases and less in others. The most drastic change I experienced was a deliverance from a recent gripping depression I had never experienced before in my life. After praying through it at the first Skype meeting, it simply vanished from my life! It has now been about three months since then and I feel like I never went through that season!

In some other subtle ways, I was seeing the way God views me during some of the worst situations in my life. He has always been there and always will be! It brought new and fresh insight as to how God is out for my good and His glory in my life. The song "In Christ Alone" has kept coming to mind, especially where it goes "no power of hell, no scheme of man can ever pluck me from His hand." Again, it's funny since I am always quick to explain how God is super involved in our lives and has a desire to love us, but I did not fully accept that full love of the Father.

Overall, this time was beneficial and freshened my relationship with God in ways I have not experienced for some time. I would not say healing prayer is a silver bullet in getting your problems fixed in a moment. Much of what we went over the Lord had been talking to me about for days beforehand, but at the right time the Lord presented His truth fully during Wholeness Prayer. I have now started counseling with a professional counselor and think this time coming will be very beneficial as I have done away with many of the old ways of thinking and put on the new ways.

Recently I have been reading a book by A.W Tozer called *The Knowledge of the Holy*. In one chapter, he describes the attributes of God as more than just the few that theologians seem to focus on, but rather something infinite that a person can spend an eternity exploring and enjoying. I believe the key to going forward from here is to enjoy God for all He is worth. Indulging in the beauty and purity of God will never get old and He will never leave me alone. All this is possible through the illuminating truth of who I am in Him and the knowledge of His love for me. Truly I am blessed!" ~D

Emotional wounds can be based on false beliefs, on truth, or on a mixture of the two. The pain of an emotional wound tends to be triggered by anything remotely similar to the situation where it began (the root). Such triggers bring opportunities for growth and healing. Receiving God's perspective at the root doesn't change what happened in the memory or pattern, but it can dramatically change how the person thinks and feels about what happened, and how they choose to respond to similar situations in the future.

Sometimes the person being prayed for has experienced abuse or trauma, or the feelings related to a memory are strongly negative. In such cases, we recommend that they pray through those issues with a mature follower of Jesus[23]. Later on, they may want to process other less painful memories on their own.

1. Emotional Wounds Based on False Beliefs [24]

Therefore, since we have a great high priest
who has passed through the heavens,
Jesus the Son of God, let us hold fast our confession.
For we do not have a high priest
who cannot sympathize with our weaknesses,
but One who has been tempted in all things as we are,
yet without sin.
Therefore let us draw near with confidence to the throne of grace,
so that we may receive mercy
and find grace to help in time of need.
~Hebrews 4: 14-16 (NASB)

Joe, the leader of a ministry team, had a constant fear that he would fail and that nothing he did would ever be good enough. When I prayed with Joe using Wholeness Prayer, God reminded him that when he was young, his father often called him a "stupid idiot." In the root memory God revealed, he saw himself repeatedly being shouted at while helping his father paint the back porch. He felt great shame in the memory. The intense false belief rooted in this memory was, "I can never do anything right."

This deception did not necessarily take root in Joe's mind the first time he was called a stupid idiot. The destructive belief became anchored in his mind the first time he accepted the misinformation as reality. It was rooted in his *agreement* with the misinformation; not in the misinformation itself.

When praying through emotional wounds based on false beliefs, it's important to identify the feelings and beliefs in the root memory or pattern. False beliefs in a memory correspond with the negative emotions being experienced. There may be more than one false belief in a memory, or two or more intertwined root memories connected to an emotion or false belief. As false beliefs emerge, they will feel strongly true (at a heart level) to the person being prayed for.

Many false beliefs are generational. If someone is experiencing unhealthy fear, anger or shame, depression, bitterness, or other negative emotions[25], false beliefs may be involved. Common false beliefs include: "I'm no good," "I am unacceptable unless I ...," "If I make a mistake, I'll never be forgiven," "I have to pay for my mistakes," "I'm so stupid. I can't do anything right," "I'm worthless," "I'm a hopeless case," "My opinions aren't worth listening to," "No one ever listens to me," "I'll never be able to do this," "No one loves me," "I'm too .... No one will ever love me," "Life is hopeless," "I can never change," and "I can never trust anyone."

After Joe's root memory was identified, together with the feelings and false beliefs contained in it, we invited God to reveal His truth in the memory. He showed Joe that He was there on the back porch, standing between Joe and his father, absorbing the harsh words and taking Joe's shame away. He reminded Joe that He is always with him and ready to help him. He helped Joe understand that his father wasn't able to mentor him well because of his own struggles with shame. Joe was then able to forgive his father. During the prayer time and from then onward, Joe was able to receive more love from his heavenly Father. He grew in security and in patience with himself, his family and those on his ministry team.

Keys
Identify
- Feelings
- False beliefs
- Root memory (or pattern)

2. Unpleasant Emotions Based on Truth

Surely our griefs He Himself bore, And our sorrows He carried.
~Isaiah 53:4a (NASB)

In less than a year, five of Sarah's loved ones had passed away. When I met with her, she was struggling with depression. Together we brought her losses to God. He spoke comfort to her heart, and gave her a sense of closure in her relationship with a recently deceased aunt with whom she'd had a strained relationship. He also relieved her of the emotional burden she'd been carrying on behalf of her sister, May, whose fiancée had been killed in an accident. Her face became radiant as we prayed, and she returned home with renewed hope.

While many unpleasant emotions are rooted in false beliefs, they may also arise from a mixture of false beliefs and truth. Or they may be based on truth, in situations such as grief over the death of a loved one, loss of a friendship, sadness over a lost childhood,[26] betrayal, broken trust, disappointments, and remorse for sin.

If the person being prayed for is experiencing unpleasant emotions based on truth, God wants to walk with them and carry their grief and sorrow.

When praying with someone through unpleasant emotions based on truth, we find the following steps helpful:
- Thank God that
  - Jesus invites us to be yoked together with Him and find rest (Matthew 11:28-30).
  - He carried all our griefs and sorrows on the cross (Isaiah 53:4a).

- Ask God to help the person being prayed for feel as much of the pain as He wants them to feel now, in His presence. They might feel this pain physically as well as emotionally. As they connect with the pain, ask God to carry this load and to help the person give Him their burden.
- Thank Him for what He has done.

God may not immediately remove all the unpleasant emotion(s) from the memory. Even if He leaves some of the pain for a time, He offers to give us rest and walk with us on the journey.

Keys
- Ask God to carry the burden (Isaiah 53:4).
- Give Him the burden (1 Peter 5:7).

3. Anger

But now you must also rid yourselves of all such things as these: anger, rage, malice, slander, and filthy language from your lips.
~Colossians 3:8 (NIV)

> "During Wholeness Prayer I was reminded of a childhood memory where I felt angry at my dad. I didn't want to let go of my anger, as I felt the only other choice was to feel worthless. I brought the memory to God, felt the anger, and connected with my belief that my only other choice was to feel worthless. Then I asked God to reveal His perspective. Immediately I heard a still, small voice saying, 'I thought you were worth dying for.' My perspective instantly changed and I quickly let go of my anger and forgave my dad. The peace of that moment remains today and the truth that God thought I was worth dying for continues to shape my life. To God be the glory!" ~A

Anger is a secondary emotion.[27] Underneath anger are primary emotions, often frustration, fear, shame and/or hurt. If anger is present in a memory, we ask God to reveal, to the person being prayed for, how they felt *just before* they became angry, even if they were not aware of this emotion at the time. It may also help to ask God to reveal to the person whether or not they feel (or think) they need to hang onto their anger for any reason, then pray through any related root issues.

Some anger is rooted in truth. Even so, we are told not to "let the sun go down while you are still angry" (Ephesians 4:26b, NIV). People are not designed to carry anger around for long. It's destructive to our bodies. And "...human anger does not produce the righteousness that God desires" (James 1:20b, NIV).

Along with praying through their anger and the underlying emotions involved, the person being prayed for may need to work through issues of judging others (page 138) or feeling judged (page 139), unforgiveness (page 101), and any desire to take revenge.

Keys
- Anger isn't a root emotion.
- Pray through the root (underlying) emotion – often frustration, fear, shame and/or hurt.

Chapter 9. Replacing Curses with Blessings[28]

Praise be to the God and Father of our Lord Jesus Christ, who has blessed us in the heavenly realms with every spiritual blessing in Christ.
~Ephesians 1:3 (NIV)

"I didn't know what Wholeness Prayer was and I didn't know what to expect, but Jean was visiting. After hearing her mention it to others, I invited her to pray with me. We chatted a bit, then dove right in. I was expectant for what the Lord would do. Jean prayed a simple prayer, then I tried to listen to the Lord, and then Jean asked what I saw/heard. At first I wasn't really sure, but we repeated the process: prayer, listening, then sharing.

Gradually a pattern emerged - I saw many of the more serious situations where I had failed or let others down, and pinpointed Satan's lie telling me that "I'm a failure." Then God replaced that lie with His truth - He knows each of those situations where I failed. But He still loves me, adopted me as His child, covered my failures with His blood shed on the cross and gives me His perfect righteousness. He makes me blameless in His sight.

While I knew all these truths, I don't know that I had specifically confronted those past failures and Satan's lie, or allowed God to speak His truth over me like that. Because I didn't know what to expect (and my failures were not on my agenda for the prayer time) I was a little surprised when my failures and Satan's lie came out as we prayed. But I believe that God knew what I needed to hear and these things were on His agenda for me that day. This was a freeing experience and I'm continuing to seek to walk in that truth and freedom." ~P

Parents and other influencers can have a powerful impact on a child – for good or ill. The person being prayed for may have been blessed by their parents at key periods in their life, whether this blessing was given formally or informally. Or there may have been an absence of blessing at some key periods of their lives, where their parents were not affirming or even cursed them in some way.[29]

Blessings can be general or specific, formal or informal. A general blessing, such as "I trust you to make good choices," is very empowering. "The tongue has the power of life and death" (Proverbs 18:21a, NIV). People who have been blessed in this way are much more likely to have confidence in the choices they make throughout their lives. Even after parents (or other significant influencers in a person's life) are no longer living, the impact of their blessings continues.

If someone has experienced neglect, or hurtful words or actions, they may have begun to live from a destructive set of beliefs about themselves. If the person being prayed for is a believer in Christ and has felt cursed (or felt a lack of blessing) at significant points in their life, God would like to help them identify those and replace them with His blessings. He wants followers of Jesus to know who we truly are in Him.

Examples

Blessings (Words of Life)	Curses (Hurtful Words)
You are precious to me.	You are worthless.
I'm so glad you're my son.	I wish you were never born.
You have a good mind.	You will never amount to anything.
You are good at solving problems.	You will never succeed.
You are doing a really great job.	You never do it right.

When helping a believer in Christ pray through these things, you may find the following steps helpful:
- Ask God to reveal to them significant times in their life when they felt blessed by their parents or other significant family members. Then ask Him to help them receive these blessings in the name of Jesus.
- Ask God to reveal to them significant times in their life when they felt either a curse or a lack of blessing from their parents or other significant family members. Then ask Him to replace these curses or lacks with a blessing. If the person being prayed for has trouble hearing God speak blessings into these places, ask Him to reveal why. Work through any issues that emerge, such as forgiving and accepting one's parent (page 107), surrendering to God any anger (page 72) they have toward their parent(s), forgiving and accepting themselves (page 113), breaking internal strongholds (page 129), and healing from emotional wounds (page 67).
- Encourage them to pray a prayer of blessing on their parents, and on their children as well, if they have children.
- Demonic elements may have gained a foothold because of a curse that has now been replaced with a blessing. If so, command them, in the name of Jesus, to go now where He sends them, and never return. Ask God to set the person being prayed for and their offspring free from any negative effects of that lack of blessing. Ask Jesus to fill with Himself any empty places in them.

Keys
- Receive blessings.
- Replace curses with blessings.
- Pray blessings.

Chapter 10. Understanding God's Character

*I keep asking that the God of our Lord Jesus Christ,
the glorious Father,
may give you the Spirit of wisdom and revelation,
so that you may know him better.
I pray that the eyes of your heart may be enlightened
in order that you may know the hope to which he has called you,
the riches of his glorious inheritance in his holy people,
and his incomparably great power for us who believe.
That power is the same as the mighty strength he exerted
when he raised Christ from the dead
and seated him at his right hand in the heavenly realms,
far above all rule and authority, power and dominion,
and every name that is invoked,
not only in the present age but also in the one to come.*
~Ephesians 1:17-21 (NIV)

Alex's father often erupted in rage toward him. It was often unclear why. As an adult, Alex fears intimacy with God. He thinks of God as an angry fist in the sky, waiting to smash him if he does something wrong. And Alex isn't sure what "wrong" includes. He knows it means sins like murder and adultery. But he often struggles to make decisions, even over which clothes to wear. He fears he'll make the wrong choice and God will be angry at him. But he doesn't know what the right choice is. He feels insecure and confused. He wants to experience God's love, but he's afraid to get too close to Him.

Children often learn to view God in a way directly related to how their parents (or other significant people in their lives) interacted with them. This correlation is strongest for the more dominant parent in the marriage relationship (the one who was the concrete referent of "God" that the child saw in the family system). For example, if someone's parent treated them cruelly, they learn to view God as cruel. If their more dominant parent behaved inconsistently, they will struggle to believe that God is consistent.

A person's faulty views of God can be changed. A first significant step is for them to become aware of how they view God, and how their view may have been shaped by their parents.

Working through the following may help the person understand how they view God:
- List three to five adjectives that describe your father's interaction with you when you were a child (e.g. compassionate, understanding, distant, cold, harsh, cruel, kind, gentle, dismissive).
- List three to five adjectives that describe your mother's interaction with you when you were a child.
- List three to five adjectives that describe how you experientially view God (not logically, but purely at a feeling level).
- What, if any, correlations do you see between how you view your father and/or mother's interaction with you, and how you experientially view God?
    o To what extent does Scripture confirm your experiential concept of God?
    o To what extent is your experiential view different from Scripture's teaching?
    o What do your responses tell you about how accurate your concept of God may or may not be?
- If there are any ways in which your view of God differs from how Scripture portrays Him, would you like to ask God to change your experiential view so that you can more fully "see Him" as He is? If so, ask Him to do this and to help you work through any related issues.

Someone may also be experiencing other hindrances to viewing God as He is. Many of these are explained in Growing in Hearing God <http://ent.freemin.org/wp-content/uploads/2013/08/Growing_in_Hearing_God_-_booklet.pdf>.

When praying with someone about understanding God's character, you may find the following steps helpful:
- Ask God to reveal, to the person being prayed for, if there is an attribute of His character He would like to highlight during the prayer time.
- If they would like to see more clearly who God truly is and how He interacts with His children, encourage them to tell God this and ask for His help.
- Ask God to reveal to them any ways in which their parents (or other significant people in their lives) reflected, or did not reflect, God's true character.
- Ask God to help them *separate* their understanding of each of their parent's (or other significant person's) character and how they interacted with each of them, *from* who God truly is and how He interacts with His children. To help with this
    - Ask God to show them other people in their life who have, to some extent, modeled these attributes of God's true character.
    - Ask God to show them which person His true character more closely resembles.
    - Ask God to show them how much more His character reflects this true attribute.
- Work through any issues that emerge, including freedom from generational bondage (page 53), forgiving their parents (page 107) and seeking healing from emotional wounds (page 67).
- Ask God to help them to grow in relating to Him as He truly is, including communicating with Him as He intends.
- Ask God to reveal to them any other hindrances to them seeing God as He is. Work through any issues that emerge.
- Ask God to remind them of any ways in which an attribute of God's character has been highlighted during the prayer time.
- Encourage them to seek related Scriptures, memorize these, and meditate on them.

Keys
- Identify misperceptions of God's character.
- Separate who God truly is from unhealthy role models.

Chapter 11. Praying Through Trauma

I sought the LORD, and he answered me;
he delivered me from all my fears.
Those who look to him are radiant;
their faces are never covered with shame.
This poor man called, and the LORD heard him;
he saved him out of all his troubles.
The angel of the LORD encamps around those who fear him,
and he delivers them.
Taste and see that the LORD is good;
blessed is the one who takes refuge in him.
~Psalm 34:4-8 (NIV)

"I first learned of Wholeness Prayer about ten years ago. This prayer ministry was marked by asking the Holy Spirit to come and minister at the origins of our woundedness, bringing light and healing into those places of need.

Shortly afterward I had an opportunity to use Wholeness Prayer. Tom, one of our church leaders, worked at Walmart with a young woman named Alice. Every night Alice had a nightmare about her brother, Steve. He had been instantly electrocuted when stepping out of his car after it hit a power pole and the energized wires dropped on top of his car. Alice and her mother were the ones to identify his charred body. Every time Alice thought of her brother, she remembered his horribly burned corpse. This was the subject of her recurring nightmares.

My friend Tom asked me, 'Do you think you can possibly help her?' I knew I couldn't do anything, but I had confidence that the Holy Spirit could help her, through Wholeness Prayer. I met Alice and asked her if she'd like to pray together with my wife and me. When we met, she told us about her nightmares. I explained the philosophy of Wholeness Prayer to her and asked if she would like us to pray for her in this way. I told her that we would invite the Holy Spirit into the original hurt and ask Him to reveal what God was doing at that time, which she, due to the trauma, had not yet been able to see.

We prayed for about 20-25 minutes. At one point I said to her, 'What is the Holy Spirit doing? Are you seeing or hearing anything?' There was silence for a while and then she started to laugh. She giggled and laughed and smiled. I knew the Holy Spirit was doing something, but I couldn't imagine what. So, I asked her, 'What are you hearing or seeing?' She said, 'I just saw a picture of my brother and I'm hearing his voice and he's calling out to me and he is saying, "Bucky, what's your problem?"' (She explained to us that Bucky was his affectionate name for her.) His face was totally unharmed, and he told her that he was okay and that she would be okay. She left the meeting with joy in her heart.

One day, about three months later, Alice asked Tom to tell me that she'd not once had a nightmare since praying through the trauma. The Holy Spirit had so powerfully ministered to her that she was no longer traumatized by the event." ~S

Stephen was the on-site manager of a small factory when an explosion occurred, catapulting a large piece of machinery through the roof. No one was injured, but Stephen was unable to function well in daily life, and had recurring nightmares of the experience. Since the explosion, every time he heard a loud noise, he would freeze in terror.

As Stephen prayed together with George, He received God's peace in each event in the trauma. When George asked if Stephen had any remaining concerns about the future, he shared his fear of sudden, loud noises. George asked God to help Stephen remember what He had already spoken to him in the scene of the trauma where the explosion had taken place. After Stephen connected with this truth, George asked God to show Stephen where He was at that moment, and where He would be in the future. Then George asked God to reveal to Stephen whether or not there was any reason to still be afraid, should a loud noise occur in the future.

Jesus spoke to Stephen and showed him that he did not need to be afraid, should a loud noise occur. He told Stephen that He would be there with him, and that He's in control and is trustworthy. He reminded Stephen that He was there during the factory explosion and no one was hurt.

After the prayer time, Stephen was freed from his debilitating fear and no longer suffered from post-traumatic stress disorder.[30]

Trauma is a "severe emotional shock having a deep, often lasting effect upon the personality"[31] Examples include natural disaster, violence, serious accidents, and abuse. People respond to trauma in different ways. Normal reactions to trauma include shock, anxiety, denial, guilt, anger, shame and grief. If the trauma is similar to any unresolved emotional wounds from the past, those may be triggered as well. Similar situations in the present can trigger unresolved past trauma. People who have been traumatized may also suffer from post-traumatic stress disorder.

A traumatic experience often includes a sequence of events. In the example above, Stephen first felt unsafe when he heard the explosion. He saw the hole in the roof, then found a large piece of machinery had been catapulted into a heavily populated area. Shock set in as he realized how many people could have been injured.

Goals in praying through trauma include
- Receiving God's truth and peace for each event in the trauma
- Knowing how this applies in the future
- Giving the burden of the trauma to God
- Being set free from any evil that was connected to the trauma.

When praying through trauma, we find the following steps helpful:
- Pray sequentially through each event in the trauma that is not yet peaceful, and ask God to
  - Identify the thoughts and feelings in the event.
  - Help the person being prayed for to think and feel as much as God wants them to of what they were thinking and feeling in the event.
  - Identify the first time they thought or felt that way. (This may be the traumatic memory.)
    - Help the person to think and feel as much as God wants them to of what they were thinking and feeling in the root memory or pattern.
    - Reveal His truth in the root memory or pattern.
- Continue to work through each root memory until it is peaceful. Then
  - If the root memory occurred prior to the traumatic event presently being prayed through, invite God to reveal His truth in the corresponding event of the trauma.[32]
  - Ask God to reveal how His truth applies for the future.
- Continue until each event in the trauma feels peaceful.
- Ask God to bring to the person's mind anyone they've not yet forgiven, any remaining feelings of loss, anger, or fear related to the trauma, and/or any other issues to work through. Pray through these.
- Ask God to reveal to the person where He is now and where He will be in the future.
- Ask God to reveal, to the person being prayed for, any related concerns they have for the future (e.g. hearing a loud noise, being touched in a certain way, seeing car lights come toward them, nightmares). If there are concerns, ask God to show them where He will be if they happen, and whether or not they would need to be afraid. Work through any issues that arise, including developing healthy boundaries (page 119).
- As the person being prayed for feels any remaining burden of the trauma, ask God to carry this, and to help them give Him this burden (Isaiah 53:4).

- Command, in the name of Jesus, any demonic elements that had a foothold because of the trauma to go now where Jesus sends them and never return.
- Encourage the person to rest and exercise. Remind them that working through trauma is a process. Suggest that they share regularly with someone who is able to listen with compassion and grace, and help them seek God's perspective.

Keys
- Work through each event in the trauma.
- Ask God to carry the burden of the trauma.
- Bind and cast out any evil spirits connected to the trauma.

1. Truth Revealed in a Traumatic Sequence of Events

Alan, a believer in Christ, was involved in a serious car accident. Afterward, he suffered from flashbacks and anxiety attacks. During the Wholeness Prayer time, God revealed several events and beliefs, both true and false, in the traumatic series of memories. These are summarized in the chart below.

After God brought truth to the false beliefs in each event in the sequence, Alan was set free. He thanked God for saving his life and the life of his friend. He prayed that God would get glory through him.

Events	Belief (True or False)	Truth God Revealed
Initially realizing the danger	"I am in danger." (true)	God was there. He kept Alan safe.
Seeing the bus come closer and closer	"No one can help me." (false)	God helped him.
The impact of the bus and car	"I'm going to die." (false)	He didn't die.
Coming back to consciousness	"My friend is dead." (false)	His friend didn't die.
	"I want to die too." (decision that needed to be renounced)	Alan renounced this decision. He chose instead to want to live.
Caring for his friend who was badly hurt	"I am the only one who can help my friend." (false)	Alan was the only person available to help for a short time. God was there and also helped.
	"I can never rest." (false)	Alan can rest. God is in control.

2. Applications to Abuse

> *The Spirit of the Lord is upon Me,*
> *Because He anointed Me to preach the gospel to the poor.*
> *He has sent Me to proclaim release to the captives,*
> *And recovery of sight to the blind,*
> *To set free those who are oppressed,*
> *To proclaim the favorable year of the Lord.*
> ~Luke 4:18-19 (NASB)

"Andy was sexually abused by an older fellow student while he was attending an Indonesian seminary. He prayed through this trauma with one of our Indonesian Wholeness Prayer partners. Now he is healed, married and works among an unreached people group." ~L, Indonesia

~~~

"I appreciated the four times I was able to meet with Ellen during our ... training. I feel that God really used our prayer times together to help free me from wrong thinking, and also from believing and acting on scripts of past abuse.

We so easily believe lies, and Satan uses these to keep us from fully using the gifts and talents God has given us. I felt in some ways stuck and asleep but did not know how to come out of that.

Having someone walk with me though prayer (I like to call it prayer coaching) and allowing Christ to come into those memories is really freeing. I no longer struggle with the same thoughts and feelings of being stuck and asleep. I feel freer than ever before and I'm growing in my relationship with Christ.

I am a mom of four children, a team leader's wife, a coach to new [expat] women and a leader in my country. I help train church leaders in discipleship strategies. I have served with my family for 20 years in Peru. I am hopeful

God can use me as I pray with other women for victory from some of the strongholds in their lives. I have not had any training in Wholeness Prayer, but I have experienced it. I would love to have training in Wholeness Prayer. I see how God has used it in my life to bring healing and wholeness." ~W

Marie was abused as a child and believed that she should never have been born. She had a constant feeling of abandonment, which led to feelings of rejection and loneliness. She felt deep shame and pain in the root memory God revealed. She invited God into this memory and He took away her shame and pain. He also revealed to her these truths: that He planned her birth, He has adopted her as His child, and He is lavishing grace and kindness on her (Ephesians 1).

In the root memory, Marie also felt unsafe, and believed that if she ever let down her guard she would be abused again. When Jesus spoke truth to her, she realized that she no longer lives in that kind of situation. She also realized that Jesus *did* protect her, even in the midst of the abuse, and that He will always protect her. She continues to work on learning healthy boundaries and growing in security in Christ.

There are many kinds of abuse, including physical, emotional, spiritual, and sexual abuse. Among other things, abuse involves trauma. Those who have been abused may also suffer from PTSD. Working through abuse and its effects is a process.

As people pray through the abuse and related issues, they can experience significant steps forward in the journey to wholeness. Getting God's perspective in related traumatic memories (page 83), giving Him their burdens (page 71), and forgiving others from the heart (page 101) can greatly help those who've been abused to find freedom.

Experiencing abuse or other significant types of trauma can drastically affect a person's view of God (page 79). Separating how trustworthy the person who abused them was (or is) from how trustworthy God is (and always has been and always will be) is part of the healing process. Finding their true security in Christ (page 155) may also come as the person being prayed for learns from relationally healthy people what a secure relationship based on trust looks like. Other important steps in recovering from abuse include forgiveness (page 101) and developing healthy boundaries (page 119).

When praying with someone who has been abused, they generally need to be the ones to invite God to speak into the root memory or pattern. Often this brings breakthroughs not experienced when the person praying for them asks God to speak into the memory.

Key for Praying through Abuse
- Person being prayed for invites God to speak to the root memory or pattern.

Chapter 12. Grieving Life's Losses

Blessed are those who mourn, for they will be comforted.
~Matthew 5:4 (NIV)

Tom and Beth were overjoyed to be expecting their first child. Then came the first miscarriage, followed by another, and yet another. Their relationship suffered as they grieved these losses in different ways and at different times.

Beth wanted to continue trying to carry a child to term, but she struggled with fear, and with feeling she was a failure as a mother. She often tried to bargain with God, telling Him that if He gave them a child, she would never doubt Him again.

When Beth and Tom tried to communicate with each other about their plans to start a family, she often burst into tears. Not knowing how to comfort her, Tom withdrew into himself. He worked long hours to distance himself from the situation, and from his own pain and anger. Beth felt rejected by his absence, and her sense of failure increased.

As Beth and I prayed through her miscarriages, using Wholeness Prayer, God brought peace and comfort. He told her that she was not a failure as a mother, and that she would bear a child in time. Tom also experienced freedom through Wholeness Prayer. God carried his grief and helped him process his anger. Their marriage improved, and they continued trying to have children. While more miscarriages occurred, eventually God blessed them with two healthy children.

As illustrated above, people grieve in different ways. This can create stress in their relationships. Wholeness Prayer and growing in healthy communication can help diffuse this tension and bring comfort.

Common stages of grief are shown in the chart below[33], although they are not always experienced in this order and some stages may be skipped. Those who grieve often experience deep sadness, anger, guilt, fear, pain, confusion, anxiety, hopelessness, and depression.

They may become stuck in these emotions, or in one of the earlier stages of grief.

Stages of Grief

(These can be cyclical.)

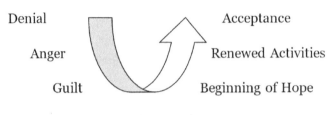

Denial		Acceptance
Anger		Renewed Activities
Guilt		Beginning of Hope

Grief and Mourning

Times of increased vulnerability are right before the
guilt stage and just after the beginning of hope.

In the grieving process, anger may initially be directed outward, toward others. This often includes some anger at God for allowing the loss to occur. Anger directed outward may then give way to anger directed inward, which includes guilt and regret. The guilt experienced may be a combination of true and false guilt.

Bargaining is also often involved, and commonly occurs between the states of guilt, and grief and mourning. "The bargaining stage may occur prior to loss as well as after loss, as an attempt to negotiate pain away....The bargaining stage is characterized by attempting to negotiate with a higher power or someone or something you feel, whether realistically or not,... has some control over the situation."[34]

In the stage of grief and mourning, unresolved or repressed guilt or anger generally leads to intensified depressive feelings. Wholeness Prayer can help resolve these issues and bring hope. As a person moves forward in the grieving process, they experience the beginning of hope, renewed activities, acceptance and joy.

These stages can be cyclical. Anniversaries, holidays, and other reminders may trigger new feelings of grief. In addition, people often become more aware over time of what and how much they've lost.

Wholeness Prayer helps people connect with God in the grieving process and work through any stuck places together with Him.

Types and Examples of Losses
- Material: *Theft, natural disaster, destruction*
- Relational: *Death of a loved one, broken relationships, divorce*
- Functional: *Loss of memory or physical function*
- View of self: *Guilt, shame, loss of self-esteem*
- Role: *Changing jobs, children growing up and leaving home, social status*
- Systems: *New work supervisor, change in the ethos of an organization, parent remarrying after the death of a spouse*
- Threats: *Disease that may lead to death or disability, talk of separation or divorce*
- Other: *Loss of reputation, perceived loss of control or sense of security, death of a dream, loss of a role model, hidden losses (e.g. loss of freedom due to the sickness or disability of a loved one, loss of a sense of belonging after a move, loss of security after a trauma, loss of competency when entering a new job, loss of access to the family home after it's sold, loss of relationships after a conflict)*
- Ambiguous losses:
    - Physically absent but psychologically present: *Family member living overseas, child going to college and living away from home, spouse working in another city, moving and leaving family and/or close friends, family members or close friends moving to a new location*
    - Physically present but psychologically absent: *Parent with memory loss, spouse after a stroke, relative who is disengaged and distant as a result of depression*

When helping someone pray through grief and loss, seek to discern how much processing the person is ready for at any given time. Sometimes it's best to simply listen, and ask God to carry their pain and walk with them. Other times, they may want to pray through places where they feel stuck in the grieving process. You may find the following steps useful over time:
- Let them know that working through grief and loss is a process. Invite God to walk with them in the process.
- Ask God to help them identify how they feel[35] and bring these feelings to Him, together with their questions.
- If they have unresolved feelings, especially of anger, guilt, fear, or depression, pray through these using Wholeness Prayer principles. Work through any other issues that arise.
- If any trauma was involved in the loss, pray through each significant part of the trauma.
- If the person being prayed for is experiencing lasting depression, ask God to show them why. Pray through the issues God reveals.
- Ask God to reveal any "hidden losses" involved, and to help the person grieve these as well. Work through any related issues.
- If the person being prayed for was unable to have a time of closure (e.g. with someone who has died, a contentious divorce or a unilaterally broken relationship)
    - Ask God to help them identify their thoughts and feelings about this lack of closure.
    - Follow the basic Wholeness Prayer process (page 8) to connect with these thoughts and feelings in key memories where the person didn't get closure, and receive God's perspective, first in related root memories (if there are any), then in the key memories where the person didn't get closure.
    - Ask God to give them closure.
- As the person connects with any remaining burden they carry related to this loss, ask God to carry this burden and to help them release it to Him (Isaiah 53:4).
- Ask God to show the person being prayed for if they are carrying the burden of someone else's pain. If they are, ask God to help them feel this now as much as He wants them to. As they do, ask God to carry this burden and help them release it to Him.

Relationship is a very powerful part of working through grief and loss. In addition to using Wholeness Prayer, if you are seeking to come alongside someone who is working through grief and loss
- Be with them. (One example of this is in Job 2:13.)
- Resist the urge to "help" by giving advice or stating truth.
- Listen actively. Watch for non-verbal cues. Reflect back to them what you hear them saying. Get confirmation that you understand what they are seeking to communicate.
- Acknowledge their grief. Validate their feelings. Don't hush grief.
- Show that you care. Be genuine.
- Offer hope and comfort (2 Corinthians 1:4).
- Encourage them to bring their feelings to the "God of all comfort" (2 Corinthians 1:3).
- Seek to help them take the next step in the process if they're stuck. Wait for God's timing. Don't rush grief.
- Encourage them to exercise regularly, if possible.

Keys
- Working through grief and loss is a process.
- People can get stuck in the grieving process. If this happens, it can be worked through.
- God wants to walk alongside those who grieve and carry their unpleasant emotions (Isaiah 53:4).

Chapter 13. Confessing and Turning from Sin

*If we confess our sins,
he is faithful and just and will forgive us our sins
and purify us from all unrighteousness.*
~1 John 1:9 (NIV)

Tony resigned from his ministry after it was discovered that he had repeatedly committed adultery. His habitual lying had infiltrated every area of his life, including our Wholeness Prayer times together. After his deception was uncovered, he declined meeting with me again and moved away. Since then, he has spiraled downward and often seeks release from his pain through alcohol.

Allen also fell into adultery after struggling for years with a sexual addiction. He immediately confessed to his church leaders and went through a process of healing and restoration, including Wholeness Prayer. He and his wife, Beth, worked hard to rebuild their marriage and establish healthy patterns. He continues to follow Jesus and pursue holiness.

Any pattern, way of thinking, or action incompatible with Biblical commands is sin. Examples include bitterness, unforgiveness, gossip, sexual sin, pride, lying, love of money, unhealthy control and manipulation.

When someone confesses their sin, they agree with God that what they did was wrong and ask for His forgiveness. Turning from this sin involves choosing and walking in a new path of holiness instead of the old sinful path. This process may include seeking freedom from generational bondage (page 53), healing from emotional wounds (page 67), breaking internal strongholds (page 129), replacing counterfeit desires (page 143), developing healthy patterns (page 159), or other addressing other issues.

When praying with someone who is struggling to overcome sinful patterns, you may find the following steps helpful:
- Ask God to reveal to them any sins that they need to confess and turn from.
- Ask God to show them anything within them that contributed to their choice to sin. Work through these things, including generational bondage (page 53), occult bondage (page 59), and any related emotional wounds page 67) or counterfeit desires (page 143).
- Encourage the person to confess their sin to God and ask for His forgiveness.
- Ask God to reveal to the person any follow-up steps, and show them whether they are ready and able to commit to these. Work through any issues that arise.
- Ask God to fill any empty places within the person with Himself, and help them not to sin in this way again.
- Ask God to help the person recognize any time they sin in the future, quickly confess it to Him, work through any related issues and completely turn from it.

Key
- Pray through anything that contributed to the decision to sin in this way (why they chose it).

Chapter 14. Forgiving Others

*Be kind and compassionate to one another,
forgiving each other, just as in Christ God forgave you.*
~Ephesians 4:32 (NIV)

*"And forgive us our debts, as we also have forgiven our debtors.
And lead us not into temptation, but deliver us from the evil one."
For if you forgive other people when they sin against you,
your heavenly Father will also forgive you.
But if you do not forgive others their sins, your Father will not
forgive your sins.*
~Matthew 6:12-15 (NIV)

> "Markus was very bitter toward his past and his father. He felt unfruitful in ministry. He believed he was unworthy to minister to others. After experiencing Wholeness Prayer, he became the most fruitful field worker in his Indonesian agency. God used him mightily in bringing the gospel to an unreached people group."
> ~L, Indonesia

Jesus says we must forgive others from our heart (Matthew 18:21-35). To forgive from the heart means to fully release the offenses and the results of those offenses to God. It involves working through any underlying negative emotions or beliefs that stand in the way. In the process, the person who forgives is also released.

Forgiveness doesn't depend on any action of the person being forgiven, such as apologizing. They may never acknowledge or own what they have done, or understand its impact on you or others. Forgiving someone doesn't mean that what the person did was right, or that they should be trusted. For example, it's unwise to continue to trust someone who has repeatedly abused you. In such a case it's important to implement healthy boundaries. These would include, for example, not being alone with the person or in any other situation where they could continue the abusive behavior.

Sometimes choosing to forgive feels impossible because a person thinks (whether consciously or unconsciously) that their anger or unforgiveness is protecting them from something worse. An underlying feeling or belief may cause them to conclude that holding onto the offense is a better choice than letting go of it. Examples include

- Believing that forgiving the person means that what they did was okay
- Believing that forgiving the person means the offense will happen again
- A desire for revenge
- A desire to have the person punished for their behavior
- A desire to protect oneself.

When someone is in an ongoing situation involving multiple offenses, forgiveness will be an ongoing need. Forgiveness is not the same as restoration, which involves both parties. It is also not the same as trust. Smart trust[36] includes a high willingness to trust, together with a high analysis that a choice to trust is wise in the situation.

Forgiving someone doesn't exclude learning from past experiences. "An attitude of forgiveness toward offenders does not mean that we release them from responsibility for what they did, nor that we should forget the offense and go on as if nothing ever happened...When the offender continues to be unrepentant, [we] commit them to God to deal with in His own way, not in ours."[37]

When someone chooses *not* to forgive the person who has offended them, they are choosing to live in bondage. This usually leads to more bad choices, more pain and further bondage. It also puts the offended person in danger of not being forgiven for their offenses against God (Matthew 6:15).

When the person being prayed for releases the offenses to God, He will take care of whatever judging, punishment or correction needs to happen. He also offers to carry their hurt and pain from the offense (Isaiah 53:4, Matthew 11:28-30), and heal their wounds (Isaiah 53:5).

Indicators that the person being prayed for has fully forgiven someone are
- They have compassion on them.
- They don't say negative things about them.
- They can freely bless them.
- They are free from all bitterness, anger, resentment, hate, and/or rage toward them.
- They don't accuse, blame or judge them.
- They don't seek repayment or revenge.
- They let go of the offense.

Indicators that the person being prayed for has not yet fully forgiven someone are
- They feel negatively about them.
- They say negative things about them.
- They curse them or hope bad things will happen to them.
- They feel bitterness, anger, resentment, hate, and/or rage toward them.
- They accuse, blame or judge them.
- They want repayment or revenge.
- They hold onto the offense.

When praying with someone about forgiveness, you may find the following steps helpful:
- Ask God to help the person being prayed for to identify anyone they've not yet forgiven, and any offenses for which they've not yet forgiven them.
- Ask God to show the person if they're able to fully release each offense to Jesus.
- For any offenses they don't feel able to fully release, ask God to reveal *why*. Work through any root issues, including any of the common hindrances listed above.
- When the person is ready, ask them to pray aloud and release each offense to Jesus.

- When all the offenses related to a specific person have been released to God, encourage the person being prayed for to pray a prayer of blessing on the person.
- Ask God to reveal, to the person being prayed for
  - His perspective on whether or not to go to the person and tell them about the offense
  - What are healthy boundaries in relation to this person
  - What response is appropriate toward this person
  - Any other follow-up steps.
- Ask God to help the person being prayed for to follow through with any follow-up steps.

Keys
- Bind and cast out evil spirits related to the offenses.
- Forgive the person and fully release the offenses to God.
- Receive and bless the person being forgiven.

Part 3. Keys for Additional Situations

These keys and ideas for praying through common struggles are designed to be used together with the basic Wholeness Prayer principles and 5 R's. They continue to fill in the general framework introduced in Part 1.

Chapter 15. Forgiving One's Parents

"Honor your father and mother"
– which is the first commandment with a promise –
"so that it may go well with you
and that you may enjoy long life on the earth."
~Ephesians 6:2-3 (NIV)

When Emily was a child, her mother often yelled at her in anger, saying things like, "Why can't you ever do anything right?" Emily felt that forgiving her mother for this would mean that Emily really couldn't do anything right.

When she was 15, Emily vowed that she'd never yell at her children like her mother had yelled at her. This worked until Emily was overwhelmed by her own children's disobedience and lack of respect. She began yelling at her children like her mother had yelled at her.

Through Wholeness Prayer, Emily was able to forgive her mother for the hurtful things that she had said to her, and accept her mother as a person created in God's image – with strengths and weaknesses. She felt compassion for her mother and asked God to bless her and help her to grow to be all God intends her to be.

Emily asked God to break the vow she'd made to not yell at her children as her mother had yelled at her. She asked Him to help her instead look to Him, follow His ways and be like Him. She also recognized and prayed through her fear of doing things wrong, which had contributed to her inability to correct her children in healthy ways. The result was increased peace and security, and a corresponding decrease in yelling at her children. No longer plagued by the fear she couldn't do anything right, she learned to navigate conflict in healthier ways.

If someone hasn't yet forgiven their father or their mother for past offenses (whether real or perceived), they may find themselves acting in reaction to the very things they're seeking to be free from.

For example
- Becoming more and more like their parent (such as becoming angry, bitter or anxious), or
- Becoming increasingly different from their parent to make sure that they aren't like them at all (such as being overly lenient with their own children, to avoid being overly harsh; or being overly trusting with others, to avoid being relationally distant).

When someone acts in reaction to their parent (or another significant person in their life), the focus is on their parent (or that significant person), not on God and His ways. This can be the result of a vow made in childhood (or later on), such as "I'll never be distant like my father," or "I'll never lose my temper with my children like my mother did with me." Or it could be rooted in a decision or desire (whether conscious or unconscious). For example, a person might feel a need to keep climbing professionally to prove that their parent was wrong when they said "You'll never amount to anything."

If a person has made a vow not to be like one or both of their parents, they may feel this protects them from becoming like that parent. Tragically, those who vow not to be like one of their parents often do become like them. Alternatively, they may become the opposite of that parent, but in an unhealthy way. There is another and much better choice: the person can ask God to help them to be like Jesus and focus on Him.

Sometimes people struggle to forgive their parents because they think that forgiving them means accepting their sin. Seeing their parent's sin as distinct from who God created their parent to be can help them to release the sin. Then they are more able to accept their parent as an imperfect person with strengths, quirks, and weaknesses – someone who is loved by God and created in His image.

In addition to forgiving their parents for sinful offenses, the person may also need to release to God non-sinful behaviors of their parent. These may include things that the person has viewed as bad or embarrassing, such as quirks or irritations. As they release these, they may find that they themselves need to ask forgiveness from God for judging their parents (page 139).

If a child lost a parent through death, divorce, or separation, they may idealize the absent parent and blame the parent who is present. Ironically, the real issue is their anger at (or feeling of rejection or abandonment by) the absent parent.

When someone forgives and accepts their parents, they are freed to follow God's ways instead of acting in reaction to their parents' ways. They become more able to love and honor their parents. They can pray blessings over them. And they are empowered to navigate challenging relational dynamics in healthy ways.

When praying with someone who has not yet forgiven their parents, you may find the following steps helpful:
- Ask God to help the person being prayed for to
  - See their parent through His eyes, and understand more of His perspective
  - Separate the good things their parent did/does from their sins and weaknesses
  - Accept their parent (as a person created in God's image)
  - Forgive their parent's sin.
- Ask God to give the person being prayed for compassion for their parent.
- Ask God to reveal, to the person being prayed for, any areas where they're acting in reaction to their parent. For each of these,
  - Ask God to reveal any unhealthy thoughts or feelings they have toward their parent, including any unhealthy vows or decisions they've made that are still in effect.
  - Pray through any related issues, including freedom from generational bondage (page 53), healing from emotional wounds (page 67) and breaking internal strongholds (page 129).
- Ask God to help the person identify anything for which they need to forgive their parent.
- Ask God to show the person being prayed for whether or not they are able to fully give each item to Jesus.

- For any items or emotions that they don't feel able to fully release,
  - Ask God to show them why. Seek God's perspective at the root of the emotions, conclusions, and perspectives involved. Refer to Chapter 14. Forgiving Others (page 101) for more ideas.
  - When the person being prayed for is ready, ask them to pray and release each item to Jesus.
  - As they give each item to Jesus, ask Him to
    - Take all the hurt and pain from the offenses.
    - Help the person being prayed for to release their parent from each offense. This includes giving up any resentment, anger, bitterness, hatred, rage, desire for revenge, or any judgment against the parent.
- When they're ready, encourage the person to ask God to break the power of any unhealthy vows or decisions and replace them with healthy responses.
- Ask God to help the person being prayed for to take responsibility for their own reactions to their parent.
- Ask God to show the person any sin they need to repent of (page 99) or other issues to work through. Work through any issues that emerge.
- Ask God to help the person being prayed for to thank God for all the good attributes in their parent. Ask Him to help them imitate the good things they see, and not the sin.
- When they're ready, encourage the person to pray a prayer of blessing and acceptance for their parent.
- Pray a prayer of blessing over the person. Ask God to help them bear good fruit from all that is good in them that was passed on by their parent.
- Ask God to help the person being prayed for to continually choose to love, forgive, and bless their parent.

Follow-up. The person being prayed for may also need to
- Grow in learning how to respond to their parent in a healthy way, with appropriate boundaries.
- Grow in learning how to bless their parent and appropriately show God's love to them.

Keys
- Objectively separate their parent from their parent's sins and weaknesses.
- Take responsibility for their own actions.
- Focus on Jesus and follow Him.
- Accept and bless their parent.
- Forgive their parent's sin.

Chapter 16. Forgiving and Accepting Oneself[38]

1. Forgiving Oneself

> *Therefore, there is now no condemnation*
> *for those who are in Christ Jesus,*
> *because through Christ Jesus the law of the Spirit of life*
> *set me free from the law of sin and death.*
> ~Romans 8:1-2 (NIV)

"I was dealing with some irrational fears which basically paralyzed me, so Jean agreed to meet with me. Over a period of three days, we waited upon the Lord until He brought up each issue that I needed to address. Each time I gained His perspective, we moved on to the next issue. The process brought healing to some wounded areas and helped me forgive myself and others. It also showed me where I had wrong perspectives, and gave me a new intimacy with Christ." ~S

If the person being prayed for is a believer in Christ,[39] they have been forgiven by God (Ephesians 4:32). Forgiving oneself is part of imitating God and living a life of love (Ephesians 5:1-2).

When someone lives with unresolved guilt or shame, they feel unforgiven, even though Christ has already forgiven them. They may feel as though there's a debt that must be paid and the only way for it to be paid is to do it themselves. The path of guilt and worldly sorrow is a path of bondage.

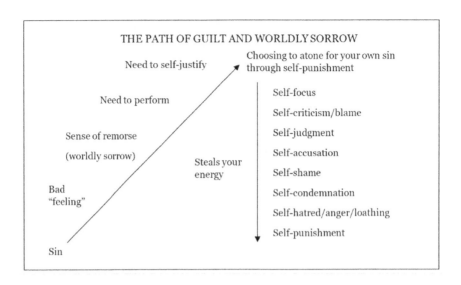

When true followers of Jesus struggle to forgive themselves, they have false beliefs about God, themselves, others, and/or the world in general. These false beliefs may have taken root as they misinterpreted life experiences or received misinformation from others. For example, a person may feel that their sins are so terrible they do not deserve to be forgiven, or they may feel they need to suffer to pay for their sin. Both of these are false beliefs connected with emotional wounds (page 67). If, for example, their parents or others said things that shamed or cursed them (e.g. "You can't do anything right."), they may have believed them.

Evelyn felt she did not deserve to be forgiven even though she'd confessed and turned from her sin. As her friend Donna helped her pray through this belief, God reminded Evelyn of her childhood. Her mother was very hard to please. She often criticized Evelyn's appearance and actions. Years later, she continued to bring up past offenses.

    In this root pattern, Evelyn connected with her beliefs that nothing she did would ever be good enough and that she didn't deserve to be forgiven. She also connected with the feelings she'd experienced during those situations: rejection, shame and hopelessness. As she did, God showed her that He was there every time her mother had criticized her, protecting her and carrying her shame. Evelyn then realized that God was her rescuer, not her accuser.

Evelyn and Donna continued to pray through the root pattern. Evelyn forgave her mother for the unfair treatment she'd endured. God restored Evelyn's hope and helped her to release herself from not being able to please her mother. God also helped her begin to separate what was actually sin (according to His Word) from what displeased her mother but wasn't sinful behavior.

In a later Wholeness Prayer time, Donna and Evelyn brought to God Evelyn's struggle to accept herself (page 116).

When we sin, God wants us to respond by confessing and turning from our sin, not by hiding from Him or punishing ourselves. *"If we confess our sins, he is faithful and just and will forgive us our sins and purify us from all unrighteousness"* (1 John 1:9, NIV).

Following the path of grace and godly sorrow frees us to experience abundant life in Christ.

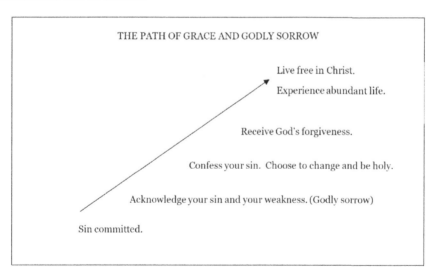

When praying with a follower of Jesus about forgiving themselves, you may find the following ideas helpful:
- Ask God to show the person whether they feel forgiven by Him.
- If they don't feel forgiven by God, then work through confessing and turning from sin (page 99) and any other issues God reveals.
- If they do feel forgiven by God, then ask God to show the person *why* it seems hard or impossible to forgive themselves. Work through the issues He reveals. This might include seeking healing for emotional wounds (page 67), growing in understanding God's character (page 79), getting freedom from generational bondage (page 53), breaking internal strongholds (page 129), forgiving their parents (page 107) and forgiving others (page 101).

Keys
- Identify why forgiving themselves is hard.
- Pray through related issues.
- Receive grace and forgiveness.
- Extend grace and forgiveness.

2. Accepting Oneself

For he chose us in him before the creation of the world
to be holy and blameless in his sight.
In love he predestined us for adoption
to sonship through Jesus Christ,
in accordance with his pleasure and will
— to the praise of his glorious grace,
which he has freely given us in the One he loves.
In him we have redemption through his blood,
the forgiveness of sins,
in accordance with the riches of God's grace
that he lavished on us.
~Ephesians 1:4-8a (NIV)

Follow God's example, therefore, as dearly loved children
and walk in the way of love,
just as Christ loved us and gave himself up for us

as a fragrant offering and sacrifice to God.
~Ephesians 5:1-2 (NIV)

Believers in Christ have been adopted by God and accepted by Him (Ephesians 1:4-8). Accepting ourselves is part of imitating God and living a life of love (Ephesians 5:1-2).

If it's hard for someone to accept themselves, this could be because they believe lies about who God is or who they really are. Some of these lies may have come from hurtful things others said *to* or *about* them. They may also have come from advertising, movies, songs, and/or other worldly sources.

In the previous section, I shared how God helped Evelyn release herself from not being able to please her mother. She began to separate what was actually sin from her false guilt and shame. She learned to repent and turn from her sinful behavior, and to agree with God by forgiving herself.

    Evelyn asked Donna if she could help her pray through her struggle to accept herself. She constantly saw herself through her mother's eyes and felt she was never good enough.

    As they prayed together, God brought Evelyn's mind back to the root pattern of her mother's repeated criticism. He spoke tenderly to Evelyn, and helped her to see herself through His eyes. It was hard for her to receive His love and believe the wonderful things He was showing her. She felt flawed and unlovable.

    Evelyn and Donna took this struggle to God, and He helped Evelyn see that, unlike her mom, He was safe and His words could be trusted. He helped her understand that He truly loved her; no amount of flaws in her could stop Him. His love for her is perfect and has no flaws. She began to open up to God, receive His love, and accept herself as a lovable person.

As followers of Jesus learn to see themselves through the eyes of God, they become free. They can live increasingly in the reality of who God is and who they are in Him. Their eyes are opened to see more of the gifts, talents and abilities He's given them. They become empowered to live in their glorious new life in Christ (2 Corinthians 5:17).

When praying with a follower of Jesus[40] about accepting themselves, you may find the following ideas helpful:
- Help them work through forgiving themselves (page 113).
- When they are ready, encourage them to ask God to help them see themselves the way He does.
- Ask God to show them any underlying reasons why it's hard for them to accept themselves. Pray through issues that emerge.
- Ask God to help them find verses that teach the reality of who God is and how He sees them in Christ. Ask Him to help them receive the truth of these verses.[41] Pray through any hindrances that emerge to receiving these truths, including healing for emotional wounds (page 67) and understanding God's character (page 79).
- Pray a blessing over them. Include verses about how God sees them in Christ.

Keys
- Identify why accepting themselves is hard.
- Pray through related issues.
- Receive God's acceptance.
- Extend acceptance to themselves.

Chapter 17. Developing Healthy Boundaries

The Lord will tear down the house of the proud,
But He will establish the boundary of the widow.
~Proverbs 15:25 (NASB)

At daybreak, Jesus went out to a solitary place.
The people were looking for him
and when they came to where he was,
they tried to keep him from leaving them.
But he said, "I must proclaim the good news of the kingdom of God
to the other towns also, because that is why I was sent."
~Luke 4:42-43 (NIV)

"Could God heal my burnout and pain? It turned out He could. Through Wholeness Prayer, God revealed to me unhealthy patterns and wounds out of which I had been living. He taught me about healthy boundaries and living interdependently [page 190]. He taught me not to fear others or their opinions of me. I learned how deeply His love truly flows. I learned it's unconditional. I don't have to earn it. I can rest in His love and know that He will truly look after me in incredible ways. My faith has been reignited with belief in an amazingly good God." ~K

Tony and Alice rented a room in their home to Evan. Before he moved in, they talked together about their expectations. Evan was very understanding of the need for Tom and Alice to have their living room be a place where the two of them could hang out together. Sometimes they invited Evan to join them, but he wasn't offended when they didn't do so.

Whenever possible, it's best to develop healthy boundaries before becoming involved in a situation. This is much easier than developing boundaries later on. It's much harder to tighten boundaries than it is to relax them. For example, it was much easier for Tom and Alice to invite Evan to join them in the living room some evenings, than it would have been for them to ask him to leave.

Areas where a person may need to develop healthy boundaries include
- Balance of work and rest
- Holiness and sexual purity
- Knowing what is their responsibility and what is someone else's
- Holding on to what they know is true, even if others disagree
- Not following the crowd into sin or unwise choices
- Developing healthy interdependent relationships (page 190).

When someone needs to develop healthy boundaries, encourage them to do the following:
- Find out what healthy boundaries are for their situation.
  - Search God's Word for relevant principles. Ask others to help them as needed.
  - Ask advice of mature believers who understand their situation.
  - Ask God to help them know healthy boundaries for their situation, while keeping in mind the bigger picture.
  - Submit the results of the above interactions to God and test the potential boundaries by His Word.
- Apply healthy boundaries.
  - Ask God to help them apply healthy boundaries.
  - Is anything within them is hindering them from applying these healthy boundaries? If so, encourage them to ask for help as needed to work through those issues together with God.
  - If someone else is hindering them from applying these healthy boundaries, seek wisdom on how to proceed, by
    - Asking God for wisdom and insight on how to proceed
    - Asking mature believers for advice on how to proceed
    - Testing their advice to see if it's consistent with God's Word.
  - Encourage them to share with someone they can trust to guard confidentiality; someone who understands the issues

and will not judge those involved. Encourage them to ask this person to hold them accountable.

Keys
- Find healthy boundaries.
- Apply healthy boundaries.

Chapter 18. Breaking Unholy Covenants

*...you took your sons and daughters whom you had borne to Me
and sacrificed them to idols to be devoured.
Were your harlotries so small a matter?
You slaughtered My children and offered them up to idols
by causing them to pass through the fire.*
~Ezekiel 16:20b-21 (NASB)

Julie initially became involved in a Wicca group through her new friend, Sierra. She was attracted by the friendliness of the people, which helped fill the loneliness she always carried with her. As she got more involved, she made numerous covenants with others in the group and with demons. The sense of power was intoxicating.

Julie began feeling increasingly empty inside. Her desire to be part of the group faded. What she had interpreted as friendliness she now saw was mere words, designed to pull her in and control her. The evil she saw in the eyes of other group members haunted her dreams.

Soon afterward, Julie reconnected with Mary, a former high school classmate who had become a follower of Christ. At first, whenever Mary would say something about Jesus, Julie would become intensely angry and cut off the conversation. Over the next few months, though, Mary continued to reach out to Julie in love. Julie was impressed by the contrast between the love Mary showed her and her relationships with the Wicca group members. Mary's eyes radiated peace and joy, and Julie longed for both.

Julie began to study the Bible with Mary, and learned of God's great love for her. Soon afterward, she decided to follow Christ. But she was still plagued by demonic oppression. Mature followers of Christ helped her pray through the issues involved and repent of her involvement in the occult. She was fully committed to following Christ, yet she still struggled with fear.

When I prayed with Julie a few years later, we asked God to break the unholy covenants she had made and shut every door to evil in her life. Through Wholeness Prayer, God helped her get significant victory over fear and terror. She became more able to receive His love for her, know how safe she is in His care, and navigate uncertainty well.

Covenants, such as the unholy ones Julie had made, are formal and binding agreements between two parties. They may be holy, as the covenant God made with His people (Psalm 111:9, Luke 1:68-73). Or they may be unholy (e.g. Isaiah 28:15). Covenants made by gang members intent on violence or racism are examples of unholy covenants. Unholy covenants may also be created through occult ceremonies, as they are in groups such as Freemasonry.

If you've been part of an unholy covenant, please ask for on-site help from mature followers of Christ when praying through these issues. If you've not yet given your life to Christ, this is the first step to freedom.

When helping someone pray through these issues, it's important to have someone back you up in prayer. We recommend that you have another reasonably mature follower of Christ present.

When praying with a follower of Christ who has been part of an unholy covenant, you may find the following steps helpful:
- Ask God to show the person being prayed for any unhealthy covenants they have made.
- Work through any related issues, including confessing and turning from sin (page 99), freedom from generational bondage (page 53), freedom from occult bondage (page 59) and cursing others (page 134).
- Break any negative spiritual dynamics behind these covenants, in the name of Jesus. Ask God to protect you, the person being prayed for and your families, in every way.
- Ask the person to pray as they feel led through Sample Prayer for Breaking Unholy Covenants (page 125).
- Ask God to show the person being prayed for anything within them that contributed to their decision to enter into this covenant. Work through these issues.
- Ask God to reveal, to the person being prayed for, any further action steps they need to take, including stopping their participation in the unholy covenant.

Keys
- Identify unholy covenants.
- Confess and turn from unholy covenants.
- Break the power of unholy covenants.
- Ask God to fill the person with Himself and protect them by His power.

Sample Prayer for Breaking Unholy Covenants (for a follower of Christ)[42]

Jesus, I confess that I sinned when I [state type of sin] and when I entered into this unholy covenant [state the covenant]. I now repent of these sins. Please forgive me.

Lord Jesus, I ask for Your protection in every area of my life. I ask You to break all the effects of this unholy covenant. In Your name, I declare that any assignments, curses or powers that were a result of this covenant are now null and void. I place the cross of Jesus Christ between this covenant and me. I reject any and every way that Satan claims ownership over me.

By the authority that I have in Jesus Christ, I now command every spirit related to the covenant I previously made to be bound in chains and be stripped of all armor, weapons, power, authority and illusions. I command that they now throw down at the foot of the cross of Jesus Christ all plans, programs, agendas and assignments that they have had in my life. I command that they now return everything that they have stolen from me emotionally, mentally, physically and spiritually. I command that they go to the place Jesus sends them.

Jesus, I invite You to fill me now with Your Holy Spirit. I ask You to build a spiritual wall of protection between any others involved in this unholy covenant and me. Make these walls as high and wide as they need to be to provide complete spiritual protection, and seal those walls with the blood of Christ.

I come before You now Lord God, as Your child, purchased by the blood of Christ. Let the blood of Christ completely cleanse me and my bloodline. I commit myself to the renewing of my mind, and I align my will with Your good and perfect will. Please show me any further action steps I need to take to completely be free from this unholy covenant, and help me to follow through with these. In the name and authority of the Lord Jesus Christ. Amen.

Chapter 19. Breaking Unholy One-Flesh Bonds

Or do you not know that the one who joins himself to a prostitute is one body with her? For He says, "The two shall become one flesh."
~1 Corinthians 6:16 (NASB)

Ethan was filled with shame over his teenage sexual relationships. He had confessed his sin many times, yet he still felt unclean. He struggled with fear and anxiety. As we prayed together, we asked God to break all unholy one-flesh bonds in his life. We also asked God to restore to Ethan all that had been lost because of his sin, and to cleanse him from any negative effects this sin has had in his thought patterns and emotions. We then lifted up Ethan's fear and anxiety to God.

God freed Ethan from the condemnation he carried, and cleansed him from his shame. He also bought peace to the root of Ethan's fear and anxiety. Today Ethan is walking in victory and holiness, and seeing God do great things through his ministry.

One-flesh bonds are created through sexual intercourse. Any one-flesh bond outside of marriage between a husband and wife is unholy. If the person being prayed for chose to sin in this way, they need to confess and turn from this sin (page 99). If the sexual union was forced on the person being prayed for or they were coerced or victimized, they may need to pray through issues of abuse (page 89), forgiveness (page 101), shame (page 67) and trauma (page 83).

When praying with someone to break unholy one-flesh bonds, you may find the following steps helpful:
- Ask God to reveal any sin that the person needs to confess and turn from. (This may or may not be present.) Work through this as indicated.
- Ask God to reveal any other issues that the person needs to work through. Work through these as indicated, including generational bondage and healing for emotional wounds.

- Ask God to break all unholy one-flesh bonds in the person's life.
- Ask Him to restore any part of the person that was lost or injured as a result of the bond.
- Ask Him to cleanse the person of any unholy thing that came as a result of the bond.
- Ask Him to reveal to the person any unhealthy boundaries they still have. Work through this issue as needed.

Keys
- Pray through anything that contributed to a decision to sin in this way (if their decision played a role in it).
- Break, restore, cleanse.
- Develop healthy boundaries.

Chapter 20. Breaking Internal Strongholds

*The weapons we fight with are not the weapons of the world.
On the contrary, they have divine power to demolish strongholds.
We demolish arguments and every pretension that sets itself up
against the knowledge of God, and we take captive every thought
to make it obedient to Christ.*
~2 Corinthians 10:4-5 (NIV)

Internal strongholds include anything within us that sets itself up against the knowledge of God. They are often rooted in false beliefs we've internalized. They are strong "holdouts" against God saturating every part of our beings. They act as a wall between us and what God wants to do in us.

Examples of internal strongholds include
- False beliefs, such as "I can't have good things," or "No one could ever love me."
- Strong negative emotions, such as self-pity, unbelief, hopelessness, worthlessness, or terror
- Unwise vows (page 132), such as "I'll never try anything new again," or "I'll never be like my mother."
- Judgments of character (page 139), such as "He's such a stingy person," (instead of simply observing "Not tipping the waiter seemed stingy to me.")
- Destructive decisions such as "I hate my father."
- Relationships based on fear (See Chapter 22 Overcoming Unhealthy Fear, page 145.)
- Curses aimed at those who've hurt you (page 134), such as "You will never find happiness."

When praying with someone about internal strongholds, we've found these steps to be helpful:
- Ask God to reveal, to the person being prayed for, any internal strongholds they have.
- When the person is ready, ask them to confess these strongholds to God. Encourage them to ask Him to break their power, including any power to deceive them.
- Ask God to put the power of His cross and resurrection between the stronghold and them.
- In the name of Jesus, bind the power of any thought patterns not consistent with God's truth.
- Ask God to show the person any related emotions and false beliefs, and to identify any root memories or patterns. Work through any issues that emerge.
- Ask God to fill the person with His truth – especially related to replacing old thought patterns where strongholds have been broken.
- Encourage the person to look for Scriptures[43] that relate to these truths. Ask God to help them to apply these at a heart level and to live in truth.
- In the name of Jesus, rebuke any demonic elements that had a foothold because of something that has now been broken. Command them to go now where Jesus sends them, and never return.
- Ask Jesus to protect the person and fill with Himself any empty places in them.
- Ask God to help the person follow through with any follow-up steps He has shown them.

Keys
- Identify internal strongholds and why these were chosen.
- Work through related issues.
- Ask God to break the power of internal strongholds, fill the person with Himself and protect them by His power.

A Few Specific Types of Strongholds

1. Unwise Decisions

We take captive every thought to make it obedient to Christ.
~2 Corinthians 10:5b (NIV)

Some of the conclusions, perceptions, assumptions, attitudes, and expectations people have were not formed on the basis of God's truth. People often make conclusions about a situation based on inadequate knowledge. This can easily happen in childhood, especially if no one helps the person get a true perspective as they make decisions and conclusions about life. They may misunderstand who God is, what types of relationships are healthy, and how to react to similar kinds of situations in the future.

Examples of unwise decisions
- "I can't trust anyone."
- "The world is a sad and scary place."
- "I need to protect myself."
- "I'll never get past this problem."
- "It's better to be angry than to be afraid."

When praying with someone about unwise decisions, we find the following ideas helpful:
- Ask God to show the person being prayed for anything within them that contributed to their decision.
- Work through any related issues, including healing from emotional wounds (page 67), confessing and turning from sin (page 99), and forgiveness (page 101).
- Ask God to show the person being prayed for His truth, as it relates to this decision. Ask Him to replace any lies they've believed with His truth.
- Ask God to help the person to apply His truth in their life and follow through with any action steps He's shown them.

Keys
- Identify unwise decisions and why these were chosen.
- Work through related issues.
- Replace false beliefs with truth.

2. Unhealthy Vows – Intentional and Unintentional

> *Again, you have heard that it was said to the people long ago,*
> *"Do not break your oath,*
> *but fulfill to the Lord the vows you have made."*
> *But I tell you, do not swear an oath at all:*
> *either by heaven, for it is God's throne;*
> *or by the earth, for it is his footstool;*
> *or by Jerusalem, for it is the city of the Great King.*
> *And do not swear by your head,*
> *for you cannot make even one hair white or black.*
> *All you need to say is simply "Yes" or "No";*
> *anything beyond this comes from the evil one.*
> ~Matthew 5:33-37 (NIV)

To make a vow is to promise to "perform some act, or to make some gift or sacrifice."[44] Vows can be made to God, to other spiritual beings, to other people, or to oneself. Even vows that are not remembered still have an effect.

Unwise vows may have been made with a positive intent. For example, "No matter what happens, I will read through the Bible this year." Contrast this with a healthy decision: "Lord willing, I will read through the Bible this year." Another example of an unhealthy vow is "I will visit at least 10 cities this year." As James 4:15 teaches us, "Instead you ought to say 'If it is the Lord's will, we will live and do this or that'."

Negative vows may have been made to God, oneself, or another person as an attempt to protect oneself from further pain. Examples include: "I will never be like my father", "I will never speak to you again", "I will never be hurt again", "I will never trust a man again", and "I will never try anything new again."

Keys
- Identify unwise and negative vows and why these were chosen.
- Work through related issues.
- Ask God to nullify unwise and negative vows.

3. Negative Scripts

> *For you know that it was not with perishable things*
> *such as silver or gold*
> *that you were redeemed from the empty way of life*
> *handed down to you from your ancestors,*
> *but with the precious blood of Christ,*
> *a lamb without blemish or defect.*
> ~1 Peter 1: 18-20 (NIV)

When Martin was young, his parents often yelled at one another. They didn't seem to be able to work through their issues and find resolution. For as long as Martin could remember, he had tried to calm them down by being cute, making jokes, or otherwise lightening the atmosphere.

His fiancé broke off their engagement after Martin was repeatedly unwilling to work through issues that arose in their relationship. This loss opened the door to Martin recognizing, through Wholeness Prayer, his pattern of making light of situations. God showed him that he often distracted others when they began to discuss serious issues. He recognized these as "scripts" he'd internalized from childhood (his part to play in the family drama). He then realized he could choose whether or not to continue to act in this way.

Some internal strongholds are "scripts" a person has internalized, often from childhood. It's as though they were given a part in a play and handed the script to use. Often children simply accept these scripts and follow them.[45] As old scripts are identified, people can
- Receive God's truth about them
- Choose whether they want to accept, reject or modify them
- Ask God for His help to walk in the new patterns He reveals.

Keys
- Identify old scripts.
- Choose to accept, reject or modify these.
- Ask God for His help to walk in new patterns.

4. Cursing Others – Intentional and Unintentional

> *With the tongue we praise our Lord and Father,*
> *and with it we curse human beings,*
> *who have been made in God's likeness.*
> *Out of the same mouth come praise and cursing.*
> *My brothers and sisters, this should not be.*
> ~James 3:9-10 (NIV)

> *If someone curses their father or mother,*
> *their lamp will be snuffed out in pitch darkness.*
> ~Proverbs 20:20 (NIV)

> *Bless those who persecute you; bless and do not curse.*
> ~Romans 12:14 (NIV)

"To curse someone is to wish calamity upon them, or to speak negative things concerning them or their future… A person can curse God, curse ourselves, curse others, or pay an occult practitioner to curse someone else."[46]

Curses can be intentional or unintentional. Examples of unintentional curses[47] include "You're stupid", "You're worthless," "You're an embarrassment to me", "You'll never amount to anything", "Why can't you be like your brother?", and "You'll be a drunkard like your father."

When praying with someone about cursing others, you may find the following steps helpful:
- Ask God to remind them of any curses they've directed toward God, themselves or others. For each
  - Ask God to show them why they chose this.
  - Work through any issues that arise, including confessing and turning from sin.
  - When they are ready, encourage them to ask God to break this curse directed toward a person and replace it with a blessing.
- Ask God to show them any follow-up steps.

Keys
- Identify ways in which the person has cursed others and why they did this.
- Work through related issues.
- Ask God to break the power of the curses and replace them with blessings.

5. Feeling Cursed

> *Like a fluttering sparrow or a darting swallow,*
> *an undeserved curse does not come to rest.*
> ~Proverbs 26:2 (NIV)

> *Christ redeemed us from the curse of the law by becoming a curse for us, for it is written: "Cursed is everyone who is hung on a pole."*
> ~Galatians 3:13 (NIV)

"Experience shows that even believers [can be] affected by others' curses. The way to freedom from curses is to confess anything that may have given rise to [or ground for] the curse, and to break the power of it in the name of Jesus, who 'redeemed us from the curse of the law by becoming a curse for us' (Galatians 3:13b [NIV])."[48]

Followers of Christ don't need to fear curses. They can ask God to protect them from all curses and their effects. "'No weapon that is formed against you will prosper; And every tongue that accuses you in judgment you will condemn. This is the heritage of the servants of the Lord, And their vindication is from Me,' declares the Lord" (Isaiah 54:17, NASB).

Hurtful words that have pierced a person's heart are an example of an unintentional curse affecting their life. When Mark's father told Mark he was stupid, Mark believed him. He quit school at sixteen, thinking he'd never succeed. His friends were amazed by his brilliance, but Mark couldn't receive their praise.

When Mark prayed through his struggle with Dave, God reminded him of his father's words. In the root memory, God showed Mark that his father spoke out of his own pain and insecurity. He was then able to hear God speak into the root memory, and tell Mark that He'd created him with a high mechanical aptitude. Mark later invented a device to better regulate the temperature in operating rooms and sold it to a manufacturing company.

If you suspect someone may be trying to intentionally curse you, pray for them and ask God to break the power of any specific curse. For stronger curses, or if you are unsure of your authority in Christ, invite other believers in Christ to pray together with you to break the curse (Matthew 18:18-20).

When praying with someone who feels they have been cursed, we find the following ideas helpful:
- Ask God to reveal anything that needs to be addressed before breaking the curse. For example, any sin they need to confess (page 99), or anyone they need to forgive (page 101). Work through any issues that arise.
- If the person feels they've been cursed because of some sin they've committed, work through confessing and turning from sin, then ask God to
  - Cleanse them and set them free from any further effects of the curse
  - Reveal to the person if there are follow up steps for them to do, such as asking others for forgiveness or offering restitution

- - Help the person being prayed for not to sin in this way again.
- If the person feels they've been cursed because of generational sin, work through freedom from generational bondage (page 53).
- Ask God to show the person being prayed for anything within them that may have contributed to their vulnerability to this curse. Seek healing for any related emotional wounds (page 67) and work through any other issues that emerge. This may include false beliefs (page 69) and forgiving the person who cursed them (page 101).
- Ask God to reveal, to the person being prayed for anything else they need to know related to breaking the curse. For example, God may reveal something related to when it happened, or how it has been operating in their life.
- Ask God to break the curse and replace it with a blessing.
- If the person is ready, ask them to pray a blessing on whoever cursed them. Encourage them to look for ways to show kindness to that person, within healthy boundaries (page 119).
- Ask God to let the person being prayed for know about any curses against them that they need to know about. These include actual and intended curses, both intentional or unintentional. Encourage the person to pray for any people involved and pray against any specific curse.
- Ask God to protect the person being prayed for from all curses and their effects and help them to walk in holiness. Thank Him for His protection. Praise Him and rejoice in His goodness.

Keys
- Work through root and related issues.
- Ask God to break the power of any curses and replace them with a blessing.
- Ask God to protect the person.

6. Feeling Judged

I care very little if I am judged by you or by any human court;
indeed, I do not even judge myself.
My conscience is clear, but that does not make me innocent.
It is the Lord who judges me.
Therefore judge nothing before the appointed time;
wait until the Lord comes.
He will bring to light what is hidden in darkness
and will expose the motives of the heart.
At that time each will receive their praise from God.
~1 Corinthians 4:3-5 (NIV)

Larry felt judged by his wife, Jennie. She was often critical of him and seemed ashamed of him. When he prayed with Sam, using Wholeness Prayer principles, God reminded Larry of Jennie's struggle with insecurity. God helped Larry forgive Jennie for her insensitivity and pray blessings over her. As Larry surrendered Jennie's critical words to God, He brought peace. Larry was strengthened to look for the truth in Jennie's words without feeling condemned or ashamed.

When someone feels judged by others, they often struggle with those implications. (This is also true if they have judged themselves.) By the power and authority of Jesus we can break the effects of any attack on their souls in this area.

When praying with someone who feels judged, we find the following ideas helpful:
- Ask God to identify any ways in which they feel judged. (It's possible that the person they think has judged them may not actually have done this.)
- Ask God to show the person being prayed for if any sin within them might have contributed to the person's decision to judge them. If there is, work through this issue.
- Ask God to show them anything within *them* that contributed to their feeling judged. Work through these issues.

- For each way they've felt judged encourage them to
  - Tell God how they feel.
  - Ask God to destroy the results of this (perceived or actual) judgment.
  - Forgive the person and pray a prayer of blessing on that person.
  - Ask God to pour blessing on them as well.

Keys
- Identify ways the person has felt judged.
- Work through root issues.
- Ask God to break the power of the judgment and replace it with a blessing.

7. Judging Others

Do not judge, or you too will be judged. For in the same way you judge others, you will be judged, and with the measure you use, it will be measured to you.
Why do you look at the speck of sawdust in your brother's eye and pay no attention to the plank in your own eye?
How can you say to your brother, 'Let me take the speck out of your eye,' when all the time there is a plank in your own eye? You hypocrite, first take the plank out of your own eye, and then you will see clearly to remove the speck from your brother's eye.
~Matthew 7:1-5 (NIV)

To judge someone in the way of which Jesus is speaking means to form a wide-sweeping negative opinion about them or their character. Examples of judging others (including God) include
- "God doesn't keep His word," (instead of "I don't understand why God did that")
- "She's bad," (instead of "She does a lot of things I don't like," which would focus on the actions)
- "He's an idiot," (instead of "That was a stupid thing to do," which would focus on the action).

When praying with someone about judging others, we find the following ideas helpful:
- Ask God to reveal to them any ways in which they have judged someone.
- Ask God to reveal anything within them that contributed to their decision to judge this person (or God). Work through issues that emerge, including confessing and turning from sin (page 99).
- When the person is ready, encourage them to
  o Ask God to free the person they judged from any negative effects of their judgment
  o Pray a prayer of blessing on that person
  o Ask God to help them not to judge others in the future, but instead to bless them.

Keys
- Identify ways in which the person has judged others and why they chose to do so.
- Work through root issues.
- Ask God to break the power of the judgment and replace it with a blessing.

8. Unhealthy Emotional Bonds

Therefore, since we are surrounded by such a great cloud of witnesses, let us throw off everything that hinders and the sin that so easily entangles, and let us run with perseverance the race marked out for us. Let us fix our eyes on Jesus, the author and perfecter of our faith, who for the joy set before him endured the cross, scorning its shame, and sat down at the right hand of the throne of God.
~Hebrews 12:1-2 (NASB)

After Todd met Esther at a party, he couldn't stop thinking about her. Unlike his wife, Esther seemed to really listen to him and understand him. The following week, he ran into Esther at a local coffee shop and asked for her number. They began secretly meeting – often over lunch or dinner. Todd enjoyed their time together more and more, and his time with his wife less and less.

Unhealthy emotional bonds can be one-sided or mutual. These bonds pull someone emotionally toward another person in an unhealthy way. More than one type of unhealthy emotional bond may exist in a relationship. Examples include
- Codependency (page 190)
- Fear bonds (page 147)
- A romantic attachment to someone who's married to someone else
- If the person is married, a romantic attachment to anyone other than their spouse
- A relationship based on gossiping.

When praying with someone about unhealthy emotional bonds, we find the following ideas helpful:
- Ask God to reveal to them any unhealthy emotional bonds they have.
- Ask God to reveal to them anything within them that contributed to this bond being formed. Work through issues that emerge.
- Ask God to reveal to them any reason why they would want to keep this unhealthy bond. Work through issues that emerge.
- Ask God to show the person what a healthy relationship with this person might look like, as well as what healthy boundaries with that person would be.
- When the person is ready, encourage them to ask God to break the unhealthy relational bond. Also encourage them to ask God to replace the unhealthy bond with healthy relational bonds and boundaries.
- Ask God to fill the person with Himself and help them grow in healthy intimacy with Him.

Keys
- Identify unhealthy emotional bonds and why they were chosen.
- Work through root issues.
- Ask God to *break* unhealthy bonds and *replace* them with healthy bonds.
- Find and apply healthy boundaries.

Chapter 21. Replacing Counterfeit Desires

*I pray that the eyes of your heart may be enlightened,
so that you will know what is the hope of His calling,
what are the riches of the glory of His inheritance in the saints,
and what is the surpassing greatness of His power
toward us who believe.*
~Ephesians 1:18-19a (NIV)

Counterfeit desires are things someone thinks they want, which really function as a substitute for deeper and more substantial longings. Seeking counterfeit desires can be a strategy, often unconscious, for dealing with painful emotions. But instead of helping to resolve the painful emotions, they hinder this process. They bring pleasure for a time, but end in disappointment.

The answer to every true longing is found in Christ. As we delight ourselves in Him, He will give us, in His time, the true desires of our hearts (Psalm 37:4). These may be quite different from what we thought they were.

God offers heavenly realities much greater than the earthly reflections. Consider, for example, the contrast between seeking earthly power, wealth or intimacy and these heavenly realities: *"the hope to which he has called you* [true intimacy, love, acceptance, and security]*, the riches of his glorious inheritance in the saints* [true wealth]*, and his incomparably great power for us who believe* [true power]*"* (Ephesians 1:18b-19a, NIV). It can be tempting to seek unhealthy control instead of trusting God and surrendering to Him. Or to pursue unholy sexual encounters instead of true intimacy, or to chase earthly riches instead of heavenly ones. But none of these can truly satisfy.

When praying with someone about counterfeit desires, you may find the following steps helpful:
- Ask God to show them if they have chosen to follow after any counterfeit desires. If they have,
    - Ask Him to show them what true desires they have that are hidden underneath these.
    - Encourage them to ask God to help them continually choose these true desires instead of the false ones.
    - Ask God to show them anything within them that makes them want to seek the counterfeits instead of the true desires. Work through any issues that emerge, including healing from emotional wounds (page 67), and confessing and turning from sin (page 99).
- Ask God to help them delight themselves in Him (Psalm 37:4), trust Him with their desires and wait for Him to act (Isaiah 30:15-18).
- Ask God to continue to reveal to them any counterfeit desires they have, and help them to replace these with true desires.

Keys
- Identify counterfeit desires.
- Work through related issues.
- Replace counterfeit desires with underlying true desires.

Chapter 22. Overcoming Unhealthy Fear[49]

I sought the LORD, and he answered me;
he delivered me from all my fears.
Those who look to him are radiant;
their faces are never covered with shame.
This poor man called, and the LORD heard him;
he saved him out of all his troubles.
The angel of the LORD encamps around those who fear him,
and he delivers them.
Taste and see that the LORD is good;
blessed is the one who takes refuge in him.
Fear the LORD, you his holy people,
for those who fear him lack nothing.
The lions may grow weak and hungry,
but those who seek the LORD lack no good thing.
~Psalm 34:4-10 (NIV)

Pete had suffered from asthma since he was a child. When he asked his friend Justin to pray with him, his life was full of turmoil. Fear controlled his mind and body, and he constantly struggled to breathe.

When Pete and Justin prayed together, God led Pete back to a memory of when he was very young. In the memory, he was frightened that, because of his asthma, he would stop breathing while he slept. Pete then realized that ever since that time he had believed he was going to die very soon. When Jesus spoke truth to Pete, Pete reinterpreted the memory to be the experience of a frightened child. He had not died; he was still very much alive. He thanked God for protecting him, and surrendered his future to Him. Now when Pete begins to have trouble breathing, he's reminded of God's faithful protection and is able to relax. His asthma attacks have decreased in frequency and intensity.

Fear can be healthy or unhealthy. Healthy fear helps people to avoid danger, e.g. driving safely and using electricity wisely. Unhealthy fear is never needed. "So do not fear, for I am with you; do not be dismayed, for I am your God. I will strengthen you and help you; I will uphold you with my righteous right hand" (Isaiah 41:10, NIV).

Like a giant tree, unhealthy fear can have many roots. Those may include generational bondage (page 53), trauma (page 83), abuse (page 89), misperceptions about God (page 79), and emotional wounds (page 67). Unhealthy fear can also have many branches, such as unhealthy patterns (page 159), a desire for unhealthy control (page 171), and perfectionism (page 175). Unhealthy fear is not rooted in truth, and cannot withstand the radiance of God's light and love. Learning to live beyond fear is a process.

When praying with someone about unhealthy fear, you may find the following steps helpful:
- If the person wants to live beyond fear, encourage them to tell God this and ask for His help.
- Ask God to reveal to the person any fearful thoughts they are currently struggling with. Pray through any root issues that arise, including freedom from generational bondage (page 53), breaking internal strongholds (page 129), and healing from emotional wounds (page 67).
- For each situation in which the person presently feels fearful,
  - Ask God to show them if they need to fear in this situation, and why or why not.
  - Ask God to show them what other response they could have to the things that triggered their fear.
  - Ask Him to reveal to them His perspective on the situation, and His way to solve any dilemmas.
  - Work through any issues that arise.
- Ask God to help the person learn new responses to things that trigger fear, and practice those responses
- Ask God to reveal to the person whether or not they feel He truly loves them and cares for them, and why or why not. Work through any issues that arise.

- Ask God to reveal to the person whether or not they feel they can trust Him, and why or why not. Work through any issues that arise.
- When the person is ready, encourage them to rebuke any stronghold of fear in the name of Jesus. And ask God to fill that place in them to overflowing with His love, protection and power.
- Ask God to
  - Hide the person under the shadow of His wings (Psalm 17:8)
  - Protect them by His power
  - Help them grow in intimate relationship with Him.
- Pray a blessing over the person. Ask God to help them grow in understanding of how much God loves them. Pray for them to comprehend how secure they are in Christ.

Keys
- Work through root issues.
- Rebuke unhealthy fear in Jesus' name.
- Ask God to fill the person with Himself and protect them by His power.

1. Replacing Fear Bonds [50] with Love Bonds

There is no fear in love.
But perfect love drives out fear,
because fear has to do with punishment.
The one who fears is not made perfect in love.
~1 John 4:18 (NIV)

Jesse tried very hard to please his father and usually succeeded. He learned to watch his father's face for any sign of displeasure, then quickly change his behavior until his father looked approving. In the rare times that Jesse failed, his father would explode in anger. Jesse struggled with fear in many areas of his life, but he didn't recognize how afraid he was of his father.

Marie worked 80 hours a week, fearing that otherwise she wouldn't please her boss. She became more and more exhausted, and came to dread tasks she had previously enjoyed.

A fear bond between two people exists when one person lives in fear of the other, and their relationship is based on fear. Fear bonds are internal strongholds "characterized by pain, humiliation, desperation, shame, guilt, and/or fear of rejection, abandonment, or other detrimental consequences."[51] "When the [relationship] is governed by fear, anxiety builds as the time approaches to be together. Fear can also develop from being apart."[52]

"We are often not aware of the fears that motivate us in a relationship. Typically, fear bonds revolve around these fears
- Fear of rejection. 'I have to do everything I possibly can to make this relationship survive.'
- Fear of anger. 'I can't stand having anyone angry at me.'
- Fear of being shamed. 'I can't let anyone see my weaknesses or faults.'"[53]

Love bonds are "based on love and characterized by truth, closeness, intimacy, joy, peace, perseverance and authentic giving."[54] Essential steps in someone making the shift from fear bonds to love bonds include
- Growing in knowing and enjoying who they are
- Taking responsibility for their own actions and feelings
- Recognizing the fear bonds in their relationships
- Letting go of both the need to control relationships and the responsibility for someone else's behaviors.[55]

When praying with someone about fear bonds, we find the following steps helpful:
- Ask God to reveal to the person any fear bonds they have.
- Ask God to show the person if they're ready to ask Him to break those fear bonds and replace them with love bonds. If they're not yet ready, ask Him to show them why. Work through any issues.
- When they are ready, encourage them to ask God to break any fear bonds in their life and replace them with love bonds. Remember that this may be a process.
- Ask God to show them how to respond to the person (with whom they had the fear bond) in a healthy way. And ask Him to help them respond in this way.

Keys
- Identify fear bonds.
- Work through root issues.
- Break fear bonds and replace with love bonds.
- Develop healthy boundaries.

2. Applications for Panic Attacks

"Do not fear, for I am with you;
Do not anxiously look about you, for I am your God.
I will strengthen you, surely I will help you,
Surely I will uphold you with My righteous right hand."
Behold, all those who are angered at you
will be shamed and dishonored;
Those who contend with you will be as nothing and will perish.
You will seek those who quarrel with you, but will not find them,
Those who war with you will be as nothing and non-existent.
For I am the Lord your God, who upholds your right hand,
Who says to you, "Do not fear, I will help you."
~Isaiah 41:10-13 (NASB)

Roger's first panic attack came just after he accepted his new leadership role. He felt overwhelmed and afraid he would let people down. It became harder and harder for him to meet with people.

As we brought this to God using Wholeness Prayer, God brought to Roger's mind a childhood memory. He'd been elected to represent his third grade class at a school event. When he got up to give his prepared speech, he looked at the hundreds of people gathered and panicked. He muddled through the speech, but felt he had let his classmates down.

God brought peace into this root memory and took away Roger's shame. He helped Roger see more of His great love for him. He encouraged Roger to invite Him into situations when he's afraid. Roger's panic attacks didn't stop all at once, but they diminished as he focused on God's faithful presence with Him.

"A panic attack is a sudden surge of overwhelming anxiety and fear. Your heart pounds and you can't breathe. You may even feel like you're dying or going crazy. Left untreated, panic attacks can lead to panic disorder and other problems. They may even cause you to withdraw from normal activities.... A panic attack may be a one-time occurrence, but many people experience repeat episodes. Recurrent panic attacks are often triggered by a specific situation, such as crossing a bridge or speaking in public—especially if that situation has caused a panic attack before. Usually, the panic-inducing situation is one in which you feel endangered and unable to escape.... Panic attacks can also be caused by medical conditions and other physical causes."[56]

When praying for someone who experiences panic attacks, you may find the following steps helpful. In addition, there may be underlying physical issues that need to be addressed.
- Ask God to
    - Protect the person being prayed for in every way
    - Bind any demonic elements and forbid them to interfere
    - Heal the person and fill them with His love.
- Pray through the basic Wholeness Prayer steps as God leads. Work through any related issues, including fear (page 145), anxiety, trauma (page 83), generational bondage (page 53), internal strongholds (page 129), understanding God's character (page 79), and healing from emotional wounds (page 67).
- Encourage the person, when they're ready and as needed, to rebuke fear in Jesus' name and command it to leave. Also encourage them to ask God to continually fill them to overflowing with His great love and to help them grow in trusting Him.
- Remind them that overcoming panic attacks can be a process. Encourage them to invite God into that process.
- Encourage them to use the following technique if they begin to panic:[57]
    - Identify 10 things you see, then 10 things you hear, then 10 things you feel.
    - Identify 5 things you see, then 5 things you hear, then 5 things you feel.
    - Identify 3 things you see, then 3 things you hear, then 3 things you feel.

- o   Identify 1 thing you see, then 1 thing you hear, then 1 things you feel.

Keys
- Work through related issues.
- Bind and rebuke unhealthy fear.
- Ask God to protect the person and fill them with Himself.

3. No Longer a Victim – Empowered by a Loving God

It is for freedom that Christ has set us free. Stand firm, then, and do not let yourselves be burdened again by a yoke of slavery.
~Galatians 5:1 (NIV)

Therefore let all the faithful pray to you while you may be found; surely the rising of the mighty waters will not reach them. You are my hiding place; you will protect me from trouble and surround me with songs of deliverance.
~Psalm 32:6-7 (NIV)

"I asked for prayer because I felt stuck. I wanted to overcome, but I often felt overcome by hard situations. I had come to see I was living the life of the good girl trying to love and serve God, though not from a place of fullness, but from a deeply disconnected and empty place.

In our several hours of praying together, the gentleness and confidence of Jean created a safe space for me. I became able to access feelings of disappointment and abandonment I had not brought to the light, but had deeply buried. I gained understanding as He began to reveal in painful memories how a root of rejection took place in my core sense of who I was. I saw that in my not knowing how to name what was happening or ask for help, I had taken on a sense of shame and inadequacy. This blocked my freedom to ask, teaching me to hide what felt less than right. Once I saw what was really happening, it was not fearful but a joy to say "Yes" to God and "No" to what bound me. God uprooted the hold of darkness, and put my feet in the path of overcoming grace.

It has been years since that light came into my soul and God uprooted beliefs that had me in bondage, opening a door to be able to stand in the grace I knew was there, but did not yet possess as mine. I believe the healing came because someone who was not afraid went with me to the throne of grace. She made requests, knowing God would answer and show me what I did not yet know how to access, and was afraid to even face. It was so powerful to have someone take my hand and walk with me to meet God AT THE PLACE OF MY DISCONNECT. I learned how to meet Him in my pain and unbelief, and there to receive and believe Him. What He began that day He continues to expand me into: the destiny of walking as an overcomer." ~B

"A victim is someone who **feels powerless,** and is therefore unable to take appropriate action to resolve situations adversely affecting their well-being. Being powerless is learned behavior originating from repeated childhood experiences where **core needs** were not met adequately. From birth and through early childhood children are unable to provide for themselves basic physiological needs, safety needs, the social needs of belonging, love and affection, and the self-esteem needs of personal worth, social recognition and having a satisfying sense of accomplishment."[58]

If the person you're praying for is a follower of Christ, they no longer need to live as victims. They have been set free (Galatians 5:1). They no longer need to live in bondage; God wants to train them for spiritual battle and give them victory (Psalm 18:31-34). They have a hiding place; they are protected (Psalm 32:6-7). They are no longer powerless; God's power is at work in them (Ephesians 1:19). They need no longer feel hopeless (Ephesians 1:18); they have been born again into a living hope (1 Peter 1:3). Their faces need no longer be covered with shame (Psalm 34:5). They have a voice; God hears their cry (Psalm 4:3). They are more than conquerors (Romans 8: 37).

When praying with someone who feels like a victim, you may find the following steps helpful:
- Ask God to help them understand that they no longer need to be a victim. If this is hard for them, ask God to show them why. Work through any issues that emerge.
- Ask God to
  - Be their hiding place and protect them from trouble (Psalm 32:6-7; 91:1-2; Proverbs 18:10).
  - Surround them with songs of deliverance (Psalm 32:7).
  - Give them *"the Spirit of wisdom and revelation, so that [they] may know him better"* (Ephesians 1:17, NIV).
  - Enlighten the eyes of their heart *"in order that [they] may know the hope to which he has called [them], the riches of his glorious inheritance in his holy people, and his incomparably great power for us who believe"* (Ephesians 1:18-19, NIV).
- If they commonly feel fear, intimidation, or other negative emotions, ask God to show them why. Work through any issues that emerge, including trauma (page 83), healing from emotional wounds (page 67), understanding God's character (page 79), forgiveness (page 101), internal strongholds (page 129), and generational bondage (page 53).

Follow-up steps they may find helpful include
- Grow in knowing who they are in Christ.[59]
- Grow in knowing their authority in Christ.[60]
- Grow in developing healthy boundaries (page 119).
- Worship. Praise. Give thanks. Sing to the Lord. Testify to His greatness.
- If they feel attacked,
  - Apply the strategy in Psalm 18.
    - Cry out to God. Ask Him to rescue you.
    - Learn to do battle in the heavenly realms.
    - Ask God to show you how to act in your earthly situation – with love, yet empowered by God.
    - Do battle, alongside God and empowered by Him.

- - Get total victory.
  - Give God the glory.
  - Praise Him, trust Him and worship Him throughout the process.
- Ask God to show them anything within them that could be part of why they feel attacked. Work through any issues that emerge, asking someone for help as needed.
- Ask God for His strategy for their situation, and to give heavenly victories. Find verses that relate to this and use them in the spiritual battle.[61]

Keys
- Know who they are in Christ.
- Know their authority in Christ.
- Know that they are protected and empowered by God.
- Work through related issues.

Chapter 23. Finding True Security

The name of the Lord is a strong tower;
The righteous runs into it and is safe.
~Proverbs 18:10 (NASB)

Whoever dwells in the shelter of the Most High
will rest in the shadow of the Almighty.
I will say of the Lord, "He is my refuge and my fortress,
my God, in whom I trust."
~Psalm 91:1-2 (NIV)

"I struggled with fear issues in my life: fear of failure and fear of rejection. I found myself needing help to live in the freedom I desired. I knew freedom was accessible in Christ, but I felt stuck in my journey. Wholeness Prayer was new to me, but I decided to try it. I met with Jean twice. During our meetings, the Holy Spirit guided our conversation to show areas of pain and fear from my childhood. During these moments, I discovered some root issues that were still causing problems in my life. Jean helped me to tune into what the Holy Spirit was doing. Through Wholeness Prayer, I was able to slow down, be still and let the Holy Spirit uproot past hurts so I can walk in freedom today." ~H

Deep down we all long for true security – to know that we're loved, accepted, and safe. God offers this to all who follow Him. He loved us so much that He sent His Son to die for us. He has accepted us in Christ. He offers true security to all who follow Him.

If someone didn't experience security in sufficient measure when they were young, it may be very hard for them to trust God now. They might
- Feel like they can't trust anyone
- Become disappointed with God when He doesn't act in the ways they think are best

- Be looking for someone to fulfill *their* definitions of love, acceptance and/or security
- Be pursuing counterfeits to seek satisfaction (page 143).

When praying with a follower of Christ about finding true security, you may find the following steps helpful:
- If they would like to grow in trusting God and living in the reality that they are safe and secure in Him, encourage them to tell God this. And to ask Him to help them.
- Ask God to show them where they've seen a secure relationship modeled in some form, even though imperfectly.
    - Ask God to show them what kind of safety and security He offers them. And how that compares to secure relationships they've seen on earth.
    - If they haven't experienced or seen a relationship that's even somewhat secure, ask God to help them to find one.
- Ask God to show them anything in them that makes it hard for them to trust Him.
    - To help them identify this, ask God to show them how they would feel if they were to choose to totally trust Him right now. And to do this with all that they are. And never look back.
    - If this feels hard in any way
        - Ask God to show them why.
        - Ask God to reveal to them where they first felt a similar reservation about trusting someone else (maybe one or both of their parents). Pray through issues that emerge, including freedom from generational bondage (page 53), trauma (page 83), lack of blessing (page 75), understanding God's character (page 79), breaking internal strongholds (page 129), replacing counterfeit desires (page 143), and healing from emotional wounds (page 67).
- Encourage them to
    - Ask God to continue to help them see more of the reality of who He is and how secure they are in Him
    - Keep choosing to trust God (as much as they're currently able to) and asking God to help them grow in this

- o Remember what God has done for them in the past, thank Him, and tell others of His goodness to them.
- o Meditate on Scriptures that show God's character and their position in Christ
- o Spend time in praise and worship
- o Tell others how wonderful God is
- o Continue to pray through any issues that emerge.

Keys
- Identify roots of insecurity.
- Work through related issues.
- Grow in knowing who God is.

Chapter 24. Developing Healthy Patterns

You were taught, with regard to your former way of life,
to put off your old self,
which is being corrupted by its deceitful desires;
to be made new in the attitude of your minds;
and to put on the new self, created to be like God
in true righteousness and holiness.
~Ephesians 4:22-24 (NIV)

Wilder et al. write, "While most of the first year of development is committed to building joy, the child over 12 months begins the important task of returning to joy from every unpleasant emotion."[62] If someone hasn't yet learned how to return directly to joy from an unpleasant emotion, they can still learn this. The section of the brain involved in returning to joy "retains the ability to grow for our entire lives. This means that "joy strength" can always continue to develop!"[63]

Some people haven't yet learned the direct way back to joy from an unpleasant emotion. They will often look for an intermediate emotion to go to, one from which they do know the way back to joy. Going to sadness as an intermediate emotion is common for women. Going to anger as an intermediate emotion is more common for men. For example,

- Dawn felt shame when her mother told her that she couldn't do anything right. When she began crying uncontrollably, her mother comforted her. Then they laughed together about an unrelated incident.
- Sam doesn't know how to get back to joy from frustration, but he knows how to get back to joy from anger. When he gets frustrated at work, he gets angry and blows up at his colleague. Then he justifies his behavior.

If someone has no direct or indirect way back to joy from an unpleasant emotion, they get lost emotionally. They tend to wander from negative emotion to negative emotion. For example,
- Denise felt deep shame when her boss criticized her work. After she got home, she yelled at her young son and hit him in anger. Then she felt even more shame and became even angrier.
- George frequently gets frustrated and wants to give up. But he feels that if he gives up he'll be a failure. So he feels he can't give up, and keeps trying. Yet he feels inadequate and becomes more frustrated. This cycle continues.

These unhealthy patterns all consist of a habitual sequence of unhealthy responses. They are an attempt to get back to joy from negative emotions. An unhealthy pattern may have many steps in its sequence, or it may have only a few. It is generally triggered by an unpleasant emotion that arises in a situation, from which the person has no direct path back to joy.

Someone might have unhealthy patterns operating in their life if
- They respond to situations in unhealthy ways, whether or not they know why
- They can't seem to change their unhealthy responses
- They don't know how to get back to joy from how they feel
- Others often react to them in negative ways. (This could also mean that the *other* person has unhealthy patterns operating in their lives.)

If someone has unhealthy patterns operating in their life
- They may or may not be aware of them.
- They may have learned them in childhood.
- They may be the same or similar to their parents' unhealthy patterns.
- They may feel stuck in them because
    o They don't know of any better way to respond
    o They know of a better response but are either unwilling or unable to respond in that way.

Knowing how to return directly to joy from unpleasant emotions facilitates healthy patterns operating our lives. Healthy patterns consist of mature, godly responses to situations and emotions.

People can learn healthy patterns by doing the following:
- Identifying people they know who have healthy patterns operating in their lives, then
    - Seeing those patterns modeled
    - Asking questions to learn more about the patterns
    - Talking through case studies
    - Role playing as appropriate to help them learn to apply the healthy patterns in their situations
- Learning about healthy patterns through books
- God directly helping them to create and implement a healthy pattern.

When praying with someone who has unhealthy patterns, we find the following steps helpful:
- Ask God to show them any unhealthy patterns presently operating in their life.
- Ask God to show them what triggered the unhealthy pattern. To facilitate this you can
    - Ask God to bring to their mind a representative time in the recent past when this unhealthy pattern was operating in their life.
    - Start with the *first* step they're aware of in the unhealthy pattern (a thought, feeling and/or reaction they had). Ask God to help them remember any other details of how they *thought*, *felt* and *reacted* at that time. Ask Him to show them *why* they thought, felt and/or reacted that way.
    - Ask God to show them how they felt and reacted right *before* that (unless they've already identified the trigger). Ask God to show them *why* they felt and reacted that way.
    - Keep asking God to show them *how* they felt and reacted. And *why* they felt and reacted the way they did. Do this until they get to the *first* step in the sequence.
    - Ask God to show them *what* triggered the first negative emotion(s) in the sequence.

- Work through any root issues related to the first negative emotion(s) in the sequence.
- If you haven't already identified the entire pattern, ask God to reveal any other steps in it of which you need to be aware. To help with this
    - Start with the *last* step you're aware of in the unhealthy pattern. Ask God to help them remember how they *thought, felt* and *reacted* at that time. Ask Him to show them *why* they thought, felt and reacted that way
    - Ask God to show them how they thought, felt and reacted right *after* that (unless they've already identified the last step in the unhealthy pattern). Ask God to show them *why* they thought, felt and reacted that way.
    - Keep asking God to show them *how* they felt and reacted and *why* they felt and reacted the way they did. Do this until they get to the last step in the sequence.
- Ask God to show them what a healthy response would have been in the *initial* situation. (The initial situation is the one that triggered the first negative emotion and unhealthy response in the pattern.)
- Ask God to show them if this healthy *response* is one they feel able and willing to choose. If so, ask Him to help them remember that they can choose this new response. And to develop the habit of responding in this way. If not, ask Him why not. Work through any root issues.
- Ask God to show them a healthy pattern that could spring from this new healthy response. (God may have already revealed this, or parts of this, in the steps above.)
- Ask God to show them how this new, healthy pattern could apply in similar situations they may encounter.
- Ask God to show them if this new *pattern* is one they feel able and willing to learn to apply. If so, ask Him to help them walk in this new pattern. If not, ask Him why not. Work through any root issues.
- Ask God to help them walk in this new pattern and find Scriptures that relate to it. Ask Him to gently remind them if they start to respond in the old way.

Keys
- Identify the unhealthy pattern.
- Find the root (the first unpleasant emotion in the cycle and what triggered it).
- Find the healthy way back to joy from initial unpleasant emotion.
- Ask God how to respond to the initial situation in a healthy way.
- Understand and apply a new, healthy pattern.

1. Example: Developing a Healthy Pattern

Old Unhealthy Pattern:

> Tryouts for the school play were just beginning. Sandra was trying out for the lead role. Though she was *nervous*, she was enjoying talking with her friend, Susan. Then she saw Mr. Engels and Ms. Barry, who were deciding who would get each part in the school play, talking together.
> Sandra felt *afraid*. Her emotions started to spiral downward. *Anxious* thoughts ran through her head, one right after the other. "I'm afraid I won't remember my lines." "What if I don't get the part?" "I'll be too embarrassed to go to school tomorrow." "What can I do?" She became more and more *afraid*.
> Sandra decided to *try to control the situation* by *pushing* herself *harder*. She told herself: "You have to do this well, otherwise you'll be a failure." She began to *panic*. When the time came for her tryout, she couldn't think straight. Though she could normally act quite well and knew her lines perfectly, she forgot her lines. She *felt like a failure*. She was sure she wouldn't get the part now. She felt *hopeless*.
> Then she got *angry* and *blamed* Susan for what happened. "Why didn't you help me practice more?" "It's your fault I didn't know my lines." Susan walked away, feeling rejected. Sandra felt *empty* and *discouraged*.

New Healthy Pattern:

After last year's tryouts, Susan had prayed with a friend about the unhealthy pattern above. It started with *fear*, then led to *anxiety* and a *desire for unhealthy control*. Next it led to *panic* and a sense of *failure*; then to *anger, blaming others, emptiness* and *discouragement.* God had helped her to identify this pattern and replace it with a new pattern. She had asked Him to help her follow this new pattern. She didn't always remember to follow it right away; but the new pattern was getting to be more of a habit, as she practiced it.

Tryouts for this year's school play were just beginning. Sandra was talking with her friend, Susan (who had long since forgiven her for last year's events). They were waiting to try out for the lead role. Mr. Engels and Ms. Barry, who were again deciding who would get each part in the school play, were talking together.

Susan felt *nervous*. She started to feel *afraid*. God reminded her that she had another choice besides trying to force herself to perform well or giving up. She could follow His pattern in Philippians 4: 6-9.

She *told God of her desire* to play the lead role, then *surrendered that desire to Him*. She also *told Him of her fear*. He reminded her that He would be with her. He encouraged her to focus on pleasing Him, not other people. She became *calmer*. She *chose to trust in God.* Then she *stopped thinking about herself* and *performed to the best of her ability.* She knew that she had done her best and *felt God's pleasure.* She thanked Susan for helping her practice. She hoped to get the part, but knew that even if she didn't, there was no need for her to feel shame, fear, or a sense of failure. She *thanked God* for His goodness and for helping her. She *rejoiced* that He always is with her.

2. **Overcoming Anxiety**: the pattern Susan used (Isaiah 30:15; Philippians 4:6-8)
   - Ask God to help you recognize when you're feeling anxious and apply the pattern below.
   - Recognize that you're feeling anxious.
   - Tell God about it.
   - Ask Him for what you need.
   - Ask Him to give you His perspective on the situation.
   - Trust your desires to Him (Psalm 37:4).
   - Surrender the outcome to Him.
   - Thank Him
     - For His goodness, and for how He's shown His goodness to you in the past
     - That He is in control
     - That He loves you
     - That He works all things together for good (Romans 8:28)
     - For whatever else He brings to mind.
   - Follow through with any other steps He shows you.
   - Keep working through these steps until you have the peace that passes understanding (Philippians 4:7).
   - Thank God for giving you His peace.
   - Ask God to help you focus on things that are pure, lovely, of good repute, excellent, and worthy of praise (Philippians 4:8). Practice doing this.
   - Remember to thank God for what He does in the situation.

3. Escaping a Looping Bowtie Pattern [64]

Sometimes two people become stuck in an (unhealthy) continuous looping pattern. Following is an example of a married couple relating with each other in this way. In this example, the husband treats his wife in such a way that she thinks she is misunderstood and unsafe. She then withdraws and puts up a wall. That makes the husband think he has been abandoned so he pursues her harder and this makes her believe that she is even more unsafe, and so the cycle continues. Included in this pattern are three levels of interaction: 1) *thinking*, 2) *behavior*, and 3) *feelings*.

	Husband	**Wife**
Thinking Level	She is abandoning me.	He does not understand me. I am not safe.
Related *Behavior*	I pursue her. I take charge.	I withdraw. I put up a wall.
Feeling Level	1) on the *surface* – anger 2) down *deep* – rejection	1) on the *surface* – fear 2) down *deep* – insecurity

Thoughts (Husband)　　Thoughts (Wife)

Feelings (H)　　　　　　　　　　　　　　Feelings (W)

Actions (W)　　Actions (H)

This looping pattern is a seamless figure eight of thoughts, actions, and feelings. One spouse's actions lead to the other spouse feeling a certain way. Their feelings lead to thoughts which lead to actions. This triggers the other person's feelings. Their feelings lead to thoughts which lead to actions. And the cycle continues. Beginning to identify a looping pattern can start at any point.

When praying with one member of a looping pattern, we find the following ideas helpful:
- Ask God to help them to identify *their own* negative emotions and unhealthy responses within the looping pattern.
  - Ask God to help them first identify what they *think* and *do*.
  - Ask God to help them identify their *feelings*.
  - Ask God to help them identify their *underlying* feelings.
- Ask God to show them if they would like to change *their own* reactions within the looping pattern.
  - Ask God to show them how they can *think* differently (e.g. about any triggers, about the other person involved).
  - Ask God to show them what they can choose to *do* differently.
  - Ask God to help the person being prayed for, to respond in these new, healthy ways.
- Ask God to help the person being prayed for not to assume they know *why* the other person initiates or responds in a certain way. (The other person may have different thoughts and emotions than one might assume.)
- Ask God to help the person you're praying for to love the other person in the looping pattern (Colossians 3:13-14; 1 Corinthians 13). Ask God to help the other person seek healing as needed.
- Encourage the person being prayed for to share with the other person involved, as appropriate, what God shown them about *their own* unhealthy contribution to the pattern.

Keys
- Identify their own unhealthy contribution to the pattern.
- Work through related issues.
- Learn to respond in a healthy way.

4. Freedom from the Drama Triangle

> *We have escaped like a bird from the fowler's snare;*
> *the snare has been broken, and we have escaped.*
> *Our help is in the name of the Lord,*
> *the Maker of heaven and earth.*
> ~Psalm 124:7-8 (NIV)

Karl's father often belittled him, saying things like "You're no good. You'll never amount to anything." Disturbed by this, his mother defended him. She'd often tell him, "I'm here for you. You can always count on me." Karl learned to depend on her to defend him, at home and at school. Now he runs to his wife, Christy, for support whenever his boss offends him. Yet he also runs to his mother for help whenever he feels like Christy is criticizing him. If Christy tries to discipline their son, Don, Karl defends him vigorously.

The Karpman drama triangle[65] is a destructive relational pattern involving individuals in the roles of victim (V), persecutor (P), and rescuer (R). These roles can flip during a conversation or over time. Once people learn to behave in one of these ways, they tend to look at relationships through that lens.

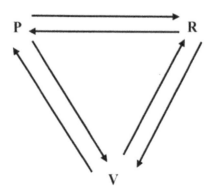

The drama triangle divides people and relationships. In direct contrast to this pattern is our three-in-one God. He has defeated the drama triangle. Jesus offered Himself as a living sacrifice to rescue us. Our persecutor is vanquished. We are protected and empowered by God.

When praying with someone who might be part of a drama triangle, we find the following ideas helpful:
- Ask God to reveal to them any patterns of relating they have that include a mindset of victim, persecutor, or rescuer.
- Ask God to show them if they would like to be set free from these patterns of relating. If they would, encourage them to tell God this and ask for His help. If not, ask God to reveal why not.
- Work through root issues, including freedom from generational bondage (page 53), healing from emotional wounds (page 67), trauma (page 83), moving from victim to victor (page 151), finding true security (page 155), and breaking internal strongholds (page 129).
- Thank God that He is Father, Son, and Holy Spirit; that He became a curse for us; that He lives in us and that He protects and empowers us.
- Ask our Triune God to break the drama triangle by the power of His death and resurrection. In Jesus' name, command all evil connected to it to go wherever He sends it and never return. Ask God to fill with Himself every place in the person's heart and mind where the drama triangle had been rooted. Ask God to protect the person by His power.
- Ask God to give the person healthy role models and help them grow in these new patterns.

Keys
- Identify unhealthy patterns of relating as victim, rescuer, or persecutor.
- Pray through root issues.
- Pray the power of the Trinity over the drama triangle – to break unhealthy relational patterns and replace them with healthy patterns.
- Learn and apply healthy patterns.

5. Applications for Obsessive-Compulsive Behavior [66]

Martin, a high school math teacher, often spent hours correcting his students' papers. He would check and recheck his work. He feared making a mistake. When he finished and went to bed, he often got back up to look over his work again.

"...people with OCD feel the need to check things repeatedly, or have certain thoughts or perform routines and rituals over and over. The thoughts and rituals associated with OCD cause distress and get in the way of daily life.

The frequent upsetting thoughts are called obsessions. To try to control them, a person will feel an overwhelming urge to repeat certain rituals or behaviors called compulsions. People with OCD can't control these obsessions and compulsions."[67]

When praying with someone who struggles with obsessive-compulsive behavior (whether or not they have a diagnosis of OCD), you may find some of these steps helpful:
- Ask God to reveal to them how they feel right *before* they act in an obsessive-compulsive way. Work through issues that emerge.
- Ask God to reveal to them how they would feel if they *didn't* act in this way. Work through issues that emerge.
- Ask God to show them whether the real issue is the thing they feel they must do or not do. Or whether the problem is with their obsessive-compulsive pattern of thinking itself.
- Ask God to give them ideas of activities that will help refocus their thinking. One example might be a hobby that they enjoy, which takes a significant amount of thought.

Keys
- Reframe the problem: the real issue is with the thought patterns.
- Refocus the thoughts.

Chapter 25. Giving Up Unhealthy Control[68]

This is what the Sovereign Lord, the Holy One of Israel, says: "In repentance and rest is your salvation, in quietness and trust is your strength, but you would have none of it. You said, 'No, we will flee on horses.' Therefore you will flee! You said, 'We will ride off on swift horses.' Therefore your pursuers will be swift! A thousand will flee at the threat of one; at the threat of five you will all flee away, till you are left like a flagstaff on a mountaintop, like a banner on a hill." Yet the Lord longs to be gracious to you; therefore he will rise up to show you compassion.
For the Lord is a God of justice. Blessed are all who wait for him!
~Isaiah 30:15-18 (NIV)

"I battled for several years with anxiety related to past events that had transpired between a fellow believer and me. Though I wasn't in an ongoing relationship with him, I would imagine difficult conversations, fear seeing him or his family, and easily feel anxious about it. I prayed about it many times, sought to forgive, asked forgiveness, and tried to let it go. But it kept resurfacing.

When I prayed about this in a time of Wholeness Prayer, God revealed to me my strong, compelling 'desire to "fix" things.' I didn't know how to fix the above situation, yet I felt responsible to somehow do so. God revealed in that time of prayer that my view of Him had wrongly been that He opened His arms to me, gave me a hug, then sent me away, saying, 'Now, you go fix it.' He spoke to me that HE fixes things; not me.

Since that time, I've not felt under the same anxiety. The issue hasn't changed, but I feel much freer to let go and ask God to fix it in His time. I am released to pray for the person without feeling a need to 'do' something. I know

now what truth to speak to myself to combat the pull toward anxiety and control. This new pattern works not only in that situation, but also in others where I am tempted to 'fix it.'" ~T

Control can be healthy[69] or unhealthy. Attempting to coerce or manipulate situations or people involves unhealthy control. Some people don't know the way back to joy (page 159) from an unpleasant emotion, such as unhealthy fear, shame, pain, guilt, anxiety, or anger. They may try to avoid experiencing this painful emotion by trying to control a situation or another person. If that strategy doesn't work, they might try harder, becoming even more controlling. If that doesn't work, sometimes people turn to perfectionism. If perfectionism doesn't work, people may develop an addiction.[70]

Unhealthy control masquerades as a strength, while it interferes with resolving the underlying painful emotions. The way out involves repentance and rest, and quietness and trust (Isaiah 30:15). It follows the path of trust (in God) and surrender (to God), instead of seeking to take control and choose one's own way.

A middle-aged man had become president of his organization and had proven himself to be very successful in the business environment. However, every time his wife raised an issue at home, he became angry. As a result, his wife learned to keep quiet, so that she would not incur his wrath. The couple lived increasingly separate but parallel lives. They avoided communication about important subjects, and tension and resentment grew.

When praying through this cycle with a friend, the man remembered that his father used to call him "stupid" when he was young. He had transformed that message into the lie, "I am stupid." Later in life, whenever his wife questioned something he said, it was *as if* she was saying, "You're stupid." He reacted with anger, but deep down, he felt insecure.

He had been hiding the false belief "I am stupid" for years by covering it with controlling behavior. The distorted message had produced pain, which he had tried to control by hiding the message with anger. Once the false belief was uncovered and replaced with truth, he was able to start really listening to his wife. He realized for the first time that she was not trying to prove that he was stupid. She was merely expressing her opinion.

When praying with someone about unhealthy control, you may find the following steps helpful:
- Ask God to show them if unhealthy control is an issue for them.
- If it is, ask God to show them what emotions underlie their desire for unhealthy control. Work through any issues that emerge. These might include trauma (page 83), forgiveness (page 101), developing healthy patterns (page 159), understanding God's character (page 79), and healing from emotional wounds (page 67).
- Ask God to help them to grow in their ability to trust God and surrender to Him.
- Encourage them to choose to give God full control of their life, tell Him this and ask for His help.
- Encourage them to ask God to
  - Gently remind them when they start to take control
  - Help them notice how others respond to them. And when that indicates they might be acting in a controlling way.

Keys
- Surrender outcomes to God.
- Seek related Bible verses and promises. Use these to pray into the situation.
- Follow through with any action steps God reveals.

Chapter 26. Overcoming Perfectionism

*I want to know Christ—
yes, to know the power of his resurrection
and participation in his sufferings,
becoming like him in his death, and so, somehow,
attaining to the resurrection from the dead.
Not that I have already obtained all this,
or have already arrived at my goal,
but I press on to take hold of that
for which Christ Jesus took hold of me.*
~Philippians 3:10-12 (NIV)

*For what we preach is not ourselves, but Jesus Christ as Lord,
and ourselves as your servants for Jesus' sake.
For God, who said, "Let light shine out of darkness,"
made his light shine in our hearts
to give us the light of the knowledge of God's glory
displayed in the face of Christ.
But we have this treasure in jars of clay
to show that this all-surpassing power is from God
and not from us.*
~2 Corinthians 4:5-7 (NIV)

Peter had very high expectations of himself and others. It was important to him to be on time or early for events. This became a significant challenge and point of contention after he married Alice. It worsened even further after the birth of their first child.

Whenever Peter and his family left the house late for an event, he became angry and critical. He recognized that his behavior toward his family was inappropriate. So he asked his friend, George, to pray with him.

As they prayed together, God revealed Peter's deep sense of shame. His father had often been critical of him, exploding in anger when Peter didn't meet his expectations. God brought peace to the root of Peter's shame. He also helped Peter forgive his father and forgive and accept himself. He helped Peter receive His great love for him, and showed him that He's rejoicing in Peter's process of becoming more whole. Peter grew in patience with himself and his family.

A perfectionist "demands of himself or others an exceedingly high degree of excellence."[71] Living in this way tends to focus on law (Romans 8:1-2) instead of grace (Ephesians 1:5). It is a "yoke of slavery" (Galatians 5:1).

If the person you're praying for struggles with perfectionism, they may
- Think that they, others, and situations should already *be* perfect
- Condemn whatever they don't think is perfect
- Be demanding of themselves or others
- Struggle with judging others
- Lack joy
- Believe that if they do anything wrong, something terrible will happen
- Not be able to acknowledge or accept their imperfections, being wrong about something, or doing something wrong.

The truth is that we're all in process. If we're in Christ, we're being perfected, but we are not yet perfect. God is rejoicing in this process (Ephesians 1:4-5), and He encourages to do so as well (Philippians 4:4; 1 Thessalonians 5:16, Ephesians 5:1).

There's a great irony in a perfectionist's unwillingness or inability to acknowledge or accept their imperfections. If someone is not willing to hear when they're doing something imperfectly, this gets in the way of their process of *becoming* perfected. When they can't recognize or refuse to recognize that they're doing something in a way that's not the best, they don't address it. Thus perfectionism hinders *actually* being perfected; it hinders the very goal it claims to seek.

When praying with someone about perfectionism, you may find the following steps helpful:
- Ask God to show them if perfectionism is helping or hindering them.
- Ask God to reveal underlying issues. Work through these, addressing unhealthy control (page 171), healing for emotional wounds (page 67), forgiving others (page 101), forgiving and accepting themselves (page 113), generational bondage (page 53), and finding true security in Christ (page 155).

Keys
- Unmask perfectionism.
- Work through underlying issues.

Chapter 27. Overcoming Addictions

So if the Son makes you free, you will be free indeed.
~John 8:36 (NASB)

When Thomas, his pastor Rick, and I prayed together, we brought to God his struggle with overeating. The recent memory that first came into his mind was of being lonely, then heading into the kitchen for a couple of cookies. He ended up eating the whole package. The emotions he identified in the memory were sadness, replaced by comfort after he ate the first cookie. This turned to self-hatred when he finished the package of cookies, then finally despair of ever overcoming this struggle.

We asked God to help Thomas connect with the feelings and beliefs contained in this memory. And to show Thomas when he first began to struggle in this way. He remembered a time when he was five years old. He had come home sad because his friends didn't want to play with him. His mother gave him a cookie and comforted him. In the memory, Thomas had associated eating with comfort and pleasure. Thomas realized that this had become a pattern in his life. And that it had also been his mother's pattern for overcoming her own sadness.

We asked God to help Thomas connect with this memory and the associated pattern, with its feelings and beliefs. We then asked Him to reveal His perspective at the root, and to unmask any deception. Thomas looked surprised, then began to laugh. He then shared with us that God had shown him a demon smiling hatefully at him from the cookie. God also helped him realize that the sugar wasn't helping him, but hurting him. The comfort it offered was temporary and followed by greater sorrow.

God then showed Thomas, in the root memory, that the sugar high was a counterfeit for the comfort and closeness he desired with Christ. Thomas invited God into this memory and the corresponding pattern. God brought peace into the memory.

We then asked God to speak into the recent memory. God showed Thomas that He's always with Him and always ready to comfort him. This was hard for Thomas to receive, as his father hadn't comforted him. After praying through this, using the steps in the chapter on understanding God's character (page 79), Thomas was more able to receive God's comfort.

We then asked God to show how these truths could apply in the future. Thomas asked God to help him consciously invite Him into every situation. And to especially help him do this when he feels sad or lonely. He also asked God to help him love His Word, and run to Him for food and comfort.

We asked God to protect all the insights He'd revealed, and to help Thomas apply these new patterns. We then closed in prayer.

Michael Hardiman writes, "Addicts in general begin by using some substance or behavior in an inappropriate way to produce pleasure or avoid pain, thus affecting their emotional state. The kinds of experience sought after are many and varied, but they have one thing in common: a desire to repeat the experience. There are four kinds of such experience: creating a feeling of elation or excitement, relieving anxiety or some other emotional distress, creating a feeling of power or confidence, and creating a feeling of connection or unity."[72]

At the root of addictions are often painful emotions from which the person doesn't know how to get back to joy (page 159). Examples include feeling alone, worthless, or unlovable. These powerful emotions may be hidden under "cloaks" of shame, denial, delusion, or blame.[73]

A common progression to addiction is: painful emotion → unhealthy control → perfectionism (or its flip side: feeling certain to fail) → addiction.[74]

People can be addicted to a variety of things. These include, but are not limited to, alcohol, tobacco, drugs, sex, control, work, pornography, gambling, on-line games, food, caffeine, and shopping.

Breaking free from addictions involves addressing painful underlying emotions, chemical dependence, and the pressure of society. It also involves identifying and addressing unhealthy patterns (page 159) in the addictive lifestyle. The diagram on page 184 illustrates these.

Overcoming an addiction is a process. A loving community can also be of great help.

When praying with someone who struggles with an addiction, you may find the following steps helpful. They integrate with basic Wholeness Prayer principles.
- Ask God to show the person if they would like to be set free from their addictive behavior. If they would, encourage them to tell God this and ask for His help. If they would not, ask God to show them why not, then work through any issues that emerge.
- Ask God to show the person if they would like to be set free from any denial or delusions they have about their addictive behavior.
  o If they would, encourage them to tell God this and ask for His help. Then ask God to show them if they really want to know whether or not they have any addictive behavior. If they would, ask God to reveal this to them.
  o If they would not, ask God to show them why not, then work through any issues that emerge.
- If the person agrees,
  o Ask God to reveal
    - Any denial or delusions connected to the addiction
    - Any demonic or destructive elements connected to the addiction.
  o In Jesus' name, together with the person
    - Strip the addictive behavior of any power to deceive the person
    - Bind any demonic elements connected to the addictive behavior
    - Command the addiction to show its true self to the person.
- Ask the person if they would like to bind the power of their addiction in Jesus' name. And encourage them to ask God to give them freedom from it. If they would like to do these things, encourage them to do so. Support them in prayer. If they would not like to do these things, ask God to show them why not. Work through any issues that emerge.

- Ask God to reveal to the person any destructive core beliefs they have, such as believing they are worthless, unlovable or alone. Work through any issues that emerge, including healing for emotional wounds.
- Ask God to reveal to the person any painful root emotions, such as shame. Work through any issues that emerge, including healing for emotional wounds (page 67).
- Ask God to reveal to the person any counterfeit desires they have (page 143), or other issues that are related to the addictive behavior. Work through any issues that emerge.
- Ask the person if they would like to invite God into the beginning of the addictive lifestyle cycle. (See the diagram on page 184. Usually people wait to invite God in until after they fall into the addictive behavior and experience increased shame and guilt. It's much more effective to invite Him into the beginning of the cycle.) If they would not, ask God to show them why not, and work through any issues that emerge.
- If they would like to invite God into the beginning of the cycle, thank God for this. Ask Him to remind them of a recent time they fell into this addictive behavior. In this recent sequence of events
    o Ask God to remind the person what was happening when they began to think about doing this behavior.
    o Ask Him to show the person what they were feeling and believing at this time. Follow the basic Wholeness Prayer principles to get God's perspective at the root – the first time they felt and believed this way. (This may be the first time they chose the addictive behavior, or it may be farther back in time. The root could also be generational.) Work through any issues that emerge.
    o Ask God to come into this recent memory (or into the pattern as a whole). Ask Him to show them where He was, and give them His perspective on their progression toward the addictive behavior. (God is everywhere all the time. He was there, but the person probably did not recognize this at that time.)
    o If they haven't yet experienced Him in the memory or pattern in some way, encourage them to invite Him in now. If they would not like to invite God into the memory, ask

God to show them why not. Work through any issues that emerge.
    - Ask God to show the person what alternatives they had in that memory or pattern, instead of choosing the addictive behavior.
    - Ask God to show the person if they feel able to and desirous of choosing that alternate (healthy) behavior in the future. If they would, encourage them to ask God to help them. If they would not, ask God to show them why. Work through any issues that emerge.
- Ask God to reveal to the person any positive action steps they can take
    - Toward heathier relational dynamics in their family of origin (and in general)
    - Toward getting set free from the physical aspects of the addictive behavior
    - To reduce any social pressure they face to continue the addictive behavior.
- For each action step revealed, ask God to show them if this is something they (1) *can do* and (2) *believe is worth doing*.
    - If it is, ask God to help them to choose this action step and follow through on it. Encourage them to ask someone to hold them accountable.
    - If it is not, ask God to show them why not, and work through any related issues.
- Ask God to walk with them in the recovery process and to give them total victory.
- Remind them that overcoming addictive behavior is a process.

1. **When praying with someone who struggles with an addiction to pornography,** you may also find the following steps helpful:
    - Ask God to reveal to the person anything within themselves that contributed to their decision to sin in this way. Work through confessing and turning from sin (page 99) as well as any other issues that arise. These may include freedom from generational bondage (page 53), following after counterfeit desires (page 143), and healing for emotional wounds (page 67).
    - Ask God to show the person if there is anything hindering them from having a healthy, intimate relationship with God. Work through any issues that arise.
    - Ask God to show the person if there is anything hindering them from having healthy, intimate relationships with other people. Work through any issues that arise.

2. **Diagram of Addictive Behavior**[75]

    The following diagram describes various aspects of addictive behavior. These include
    - Destructive core concepts such as feeling alone, worthless, or unlovable
    - The pull toward a chemical high (instead of seeking joy in healthy ways)
    - Roots embedded in family dysfunction, personal trauma, and/or an addictive society
    - Cloaks of shame, denial, delusion or blame. These hinder the person from recognizing or taking responsibility for their addiction
    - A cyclical addictive lifestyle pattern of fantasy, ritual, keeping the lid on, and further shame and guilt.

THE ADDICTIVE MIND-SET

Destructive Core Concepts:
- Worthless
- Unlovable
- Alone
- Chemical high

THE ADDICTIVE ROOT

1. Family Dysfunction
2. Personal Trauma
3. An Addictive Society

THE ADDICTIVE LIFESTYLE

Fantasy → Ritual → Keeping the lid on → Further shame and guilt →

THE ADDICTIVE CLOAK

- Shame
- Denial
- Delusion
- Blame

3. **Keys for Overcoming Addictions**
   - Identify related root emotions, family patterns, social pressure and/or longing for connection.
   - Identify addictive roots, cloaks, patterns and mindsets, and invite God in.
   - Process, practice and pray through with God until total victory is reached.

4. **Applications to Eating Disorders**

There are many types of eating disorders. These include overeating, anorexia, bulimia, and specific food addictions (such as addictions to caffeine, sweets, chocolate and diet soda).

When praying with someone who struggles with an eating disorder, you may find the following steps helpful:
- Ask God to show the person if they have an eating disorder or food addiction. If they have an addiction, see ideas for praying with someone who struggles with an addiction (page 181).
- If so, ask God to show them if they want to be healed of this disorder or addiction. If not, ask God to show them why not, and work through any issues that arise. If so, encourage them to ask God to heal them.
- Ask God to show them a recent time they acted on this (by overeating, etc.)
  - Then ask God to show them how they feel *right before* they do this.
  - Then ask God to show them how they would feel if they didn't do this.
- Ask God to remind them of the first time they did this.
  - Then ask God to show them how they felt right before they did this.
  - Then ask God to show them how they would have felt if they hadn't done this.
- Then ask God to show them what triggered their feeling the way they did right before they acted in this way (overeating, etc.)

- Follow basic Wholeness Prayer steps, asking God to reveal His perspective in this root place. Then ask Him to show them how else they could have responded to this trigger and what new pattern of behavior they could choose instead. Work through any issues that emerge, including generational bondage (page 53), internal strongholds (page 129), negative scripts (page 133), developing healthy patterns (page 159), overcoming unhealthy fear (page 145), finding true security (page 155), and healing from emotional wounds (page 67).
- Ask God to walk with them in the recovery process and to give them total victory.
- Encourage them to persevere.

Keys for Overcoming Eating Disorders
- Identify root issues and triggers.
- Work through related issues.
- Persevere.

Chapter 28. Addressing Unhealthy Relationship Styles

Lord, you alone are my portion and my cup;
you make my lot secure.
The boundary lines have fallen for me in pleasant places;
surely I have a delightful inheritance.
I will praise the Lord, who counsels me;
even at night my heart instructs me.
I keep my eyes always on the Lord.
With him at my right hand, I will not be shaken.
Therefore my heart is glad and my tongue rejoices;
my body also will rest secure,
because you will not abandon me to the realm of the dead,
nor will you let your faithful one see decay.
You make known to me the path of life;
you will fill me with joy in your presence,
with eternal pleasures at your right hand.
~Psalm 16:5-11 (NIV)

"I recently looked over the past year, and one thing I can testify to with all my heart is that the Orphan spirit has lost its power over me. A key component to that took place during a Wholeness Prayer session over Skype. I shared some recent struggles. After praying through my feelings, we asked Jesus to show me where He was in the root memory. I saw Him sitting next to me on my bed, ready to listen to me and help me resolve my troubles.

But I was so used to having to take care of myself that I didn't even think of asking Him. I saw that it actually hurts His feelings when I don't give Him a chance to show me how powerful and amazing He is. I felt His pain. Since then I have started coming to Him with every little thing, whenever I remember. He has been answering and I am amazed.

> This is what I do with my troubles now: I first thank God for something in connection with the situation, then I say *out loud* what worries me, then I state my requests (e.g. ask for opposites of what I am afraid of) and then I thank Him that He is going to do something about it. After that, I face the challenge the best way I can. I know an invisible hand is clearing the path before me. And, over time, I usually see that He has faithfully answered those things I asked Him for.
>
> I am no longer an orphan trying to do my best to earn love, but a BELOVED daughter and bride. I delight in the amazing Father and Husband I have. I have seen this manifested in my work. I am now much better at saying "no" and not jumping at every need I see. My life has become more restful, though I still have a long way to go."
> ~I

All people desire to experience joy. Joy can be described as deep gladness and delight. Wilder, et al. write, "In a child's first two years, the desire to experience joy in loving relationships is the most powerful force in life. In fact, some neurologists now say that the basic human need is to be the 'sparkle in someone's eyes.'...

Wonderfully enough, that innocent, pure desire that begins in childhood continues throughout life. Life makes sense and is empowered by joy when people are in relationship with those who love them and are sincerely 'glad to be with them.'... Joy also comes from being in relationship with God. Throughout the Bible it is established that a powerful joy comes from a relationship with God who knows everything about me and is still 'as-glad-as-glad-can-get' to be with me."[76]

Children who grow up in a secure environment normally learn to develop secure relationships with others. They grow in relating in interdependent ways, with mutual healthy reliance on others. They generally view themselves and others in positive ways.

When children don't experience this basic security, they develop insecure relational attachments which may be dismissive-avoidant, anxious-ambivalent, or disorganized (fearful-avoidant).[77]
- People with a dismissive-avoidant relationship style often struggle with connecting at an emotional level. They find it difficult to share their private thoughts and feelings, and nonsexual touch. They've learned to take care of themselves, but not to open themselves up to others. Often they relate in ways that are independent, focusing more on self than on others.
- At the core of the anxious-ambivalent relationship style is fear of abandonment. People with this relationship style tend to have two core beliefs: "I'm poor at getting the love and comfort I need," and "I have to please my loved ones, or I will be worthless and unlovable." They view themselves in a negative light, and look to others to meet their needs. At the same time, they fear these needs will go unmet. They might relate in ways that are dependent (one-sided reliance on others), codependent (a dysfunctional excessive-helping relationship), enmeshed (each person is overly connected to the other; boundaries are permeable, limitless or unclear), or counter-dependent (acting in reaction to another's dysfunction).
- The disorganized (fearful-avoidant) attachment style is characterized by a negative view of both oneself and others. Those in this group tend to shift among the three attachment styles above (secure, dismissive-avoidant, anxious-ambivalent) without warning.

Examples of insecure relationships include the following
- A mother who is distant from her husband, but shares deeply with her 10-year-old son. (The son feels important because he's helping his mother. The mother has an outlet for emotional intimacy.)
- A husband and wife who mutually agree that one spouse has an unequal responsibility for meeting the other's needs (This agreement is often implicit.)
- An alcoholic husband and his wife, who both pretend he doesn't have this problem
- A person who exerts unhealthy control over another person.

Insecure relationship styles can change into a secure relationship style. This process is facilitated by God identifying and speaking healing into core places in the person's life. Being part of a healthy relational community can greatly help this process.

When praying with someone involved in an unhealthy relational system, you may find the following steps helpful:
- Encourage them to ask God to show them if they generally relate to people in healthy or unhealthy ways.
- As unhealthy relationship patterns emerge, ask God to show them if they would like to invite God into these patterns.
  - If they would like to invite God into these unhealthy patterns, encourage them to pray aloud and
    - Invite God into these unhealthy patterns
    - Ask God to break the power of these unhealthy patterns and bring healthy relational patterns in their place.
  - If they would not like to invite God into these unhealthy patterns, ask them if they would like to know why not.
    - If they would like to know, encourage them to ask God to show them this.
    - If they would not, ask them if they would like God to show them why not. If they are willing, continue to follow this process. Do so until it becomes clear what is at the root of their hesitation.
    - Work through root issues that emerge.
- If the person agrees with this prayer, ask God to bind all evil related to these unhealthy relationship patterns. Also ask Him to not allow evil forces to interfere with the healing process.
- Encourage the person to pray through issues of generational bondage (page 53).

These next steps are an interrelated process, as well as a series of choices.
- Ask God to show the person if they would like to ask Him to help them connect well with Him, themselves, and others.
  - If they would, encourage them to ask God to do this.
  - If they would not, ask them if they would like God to show them why not. As long they are willing, continue this

process. Do so until it's clear what is at the root of their hesitation.
    - Work through root issues that emerge.
- When the person is ready, encourage them to ask God to break any unhealthy relational bonds and patterns in their life. (If they are in a marriage with unhealthy relationship styles, it can be extremely powerful to pray to break these bonds together with their spouse. But if their spouse is not yet ready to do this, encourage the person not to wait!)
- Ask God to show the person being prayed for their present status related to trusting in God and surrendering to Him. Work through any related issues, including understanding God's character (page 79) and healing from emotional wounds (page 67).
- Ask God to reveal to the person any unhealthy behavioral patterns they have (page 159). Ask God to reveal the roots of these unhealthy patterns in their lives. Pray through issues that emerge. These may include dysfunctional family patterns (page 189), finding true security (page 155), grieving life's losses (page 93), praying through trauma (page 83), developing healthy boundaries (page 119) and overcoming addictions (page 179).
- Ask God to show the person any burdens they're carrying, including those they're carrying on behalf of someone else.
    - Then ask God to help them feel as much of the burden as He wants them to, for a moment in His presence.
    - As they do, ask God to come and carry their burdens, and to help them release their burdens to Him. (See "Unpleasant Emotions based on Truth," page 71.)
- Ask God to build in them, through the power of the resurrection
    - Healthy patterns, including true biblical definitions of words such as trust and surrender
    - Healthy boundaries
    - A healthy understanding of who God is and how life works
    - A healthy identity in Him
    - Healthy communication skills
    - Healthy conflict resolution skills.
- Command any evil that has been involved to go now, where Jesus sends it, and never return.

- Ask God to protect this person by His power, fill them with His Spirit and help them to be fully aligned with Him.

Keys
- Identify unhealthy relationship styles and patterns.
- Work through root issues.
- Grow toward relating in healthy ways with God, oneself and others.

Part 4. Applications to a Variety of Contexts

Part 4 discusses applications of Wholeness Prayer in a variety of individual and group contexts.

Chapter 29. The 5 R's in Multiple Spheres

Pray, then, in this way: "Our Father who is in heaven,
Hallowed be Your name.
Your kingdom come. Your will be done, On earth as it is in heaven.
Give us this day our daily bread.
And forgive us our debts, as we also have forgiven our debtors.
And do not lead us into temptation, but deliver us from evil.
[For Yours is the kingdom and the power and the glory forever.
Amen."]
~Matthew 6:9-13 (NASB)

The basic 5 R's of Wholeness Prayer – Recognize, Recent, Root, Receive, Renew – are described in Parts 1, 2, and 3 of this book. Using these 5 R's facilitates Kingdom breakthroughs in spiritual and emotional stuck places. Followers of Christ are set free from generational bondage, restored and transformed. They become more able to positively affect relationships and group dynamics.

After learning the 5 R's, a Ugandan pastor offered the insight that these same principles are at the heart of the gospel. God helps us to *recognize* our need for a savior and acknowledge our *recent* and *root* sin. He has already paid the price for the *root* of our sinfulness, and made provision for us to *receive* a new heart and walk in *renew*ed life.

His observation opened my eyes to other spheres where the 5 R's apply. One example is when we are asking God to tear down strongholds in a place, area, or people group. First we *recognize* these strongholds and their *recent* effects in our lives, families, and communities. Then we can join together and ask God to reveal any *roots*. After that we can ask Him to remove the strongholds – from their roots - and plant Kingdom opposites in their place. Examples include changes from oppression to empowerment, from death to life, from fear to love, from doubt and unbelief to faith. As these

Kingdom seeds are *received*, take root and bear fruit, *renew*al comes.

An article in Harvard Business Review describes the Toyota Production system. It is considered the gold standard approach in manufacturing.[78] The 5 R's are quite similar to the "automation with a human touch" process. This process incorporates one additional R implicit in Wholeness Prayer: Rest (pause to identify and address the problem at its root):
- "A machine detects a problem and communicates it. [Recognize]
- A situation deviates from the normal workflow. [Recent]
- The line is stopped. [Rest]
- Manager/supervisor removes the cause of the problem. [Root, Receive]
- Improvements [are] incorporated into the standard workflow. [Renew]
- Good products can be produced."[79] [Renew]

Batista explains, "While we have to change the terminology a bit, this concept can be applied quite readily to almost any interpersonal interaction, from a one-on-one conversation to a fairly large meeting. Here's how I've seen [it] work in high-functioning systems:
- The people involved are trained to sense and respond to communication problems, both conceptual and emotional. [Recognize]
- A communication problem disrupts the normal workflow of the interaction. [Recent]
- Anyone involved in the process is empowered to stop the forward progress of interaction toward its current goal (such as an agenda item). [Rest]
- Everyone involved in the interaction is invited to talk about the communication problem (a meta-conversation, if you will). [Root]
- Improvements in communication (at both the one-on-one and group levels) are identified and implemented. [Receive, Renew]
- Better interactions can be had."[80] [Renew]

The article then offers "three ways to apply these ideas:
- Establish norms that help the group both acknowledge and regulate emotion. [This is key to Wholeness Prayer.] (And be aware that a collection of emotionally intelligent people don't automatically comprise an emotionally intelligent *group*.)
- Make it explicitly acceptable for anyone to pause the conversation in order to assess how it's going. (Sometimes 'talking about how we're talking' is the very best use of the group's time.)
- Finally, recognize that these interventions work most effectively in a feedback-rich culture."[81]

Spheres of production, interpersonal relationships, and group dynamics all can benefit greatly from the 5 R's. Distilled into their essence, these 5 R's describe the basic process for identifying and overcoming obstacles.

Adding the main Wholeness Prayer principle of "follow Jesus" to these 5 R's exponentially increases their potential for bearing good fruit in every arena. One additional implied R has been added to the Keys below: Rejoice, which is included in the 5th R: Renew (page 11).

Keys
- Recognize
- Recent
- [Rest]
- Root
- Receive
- Renew
- [Rejoice]

Chapter 30. Applications for Physical Healing

*...the blind receive sight and the lame walk,
the lepers are cleansed and the deaf hear,
the dead are raised up,
and the poor have the gospel preached to them.*
~Matthew 11:5 (NASB)

Much has been written on the subject of physical healing, both practically and theologically. I've benefitted greatly from the ideas and insights of those who've gone before me. I will not attempt to recreate or summarize their teaching here. Instead, I will simply suggest *applications* of Wholeness Prayer that you might find helpful as you pray for people's physical healing.

Last year, my colleague and I travelled to South Asia to give Wholeness Prayer training to local followers of Christ. Many of them were first generation believers from Hindu or Buddhist backgrounds. We prayed for them and with them, and they prayed for one another. As a foundation to our prayers we asked God to give them freedom from generational bondage and territorial spirits. God moved in power, healing many – physically, spiritually and emotionally, often before we asked Him to! He delights in lavishing His love on us.

God is pouring out His power and glory in our world. Many have been physically healed as followers of Jesus have asked for this in His name. People have often been healed as believers live lives of joy and worship, and ask God to release His goodness through them when they pray.

Sometimes a prayer session includes a time of listening to God. We ask him to reveal any other issues that need to be prayed through before praying for physical healing.

When praying with someone for physical healing, you may find the following Wholeness Prayer applications helpful:

- Remember the main goal: *Follow Jesus.* Ask Him how to pray and surrender the results to Him.
- When possible, pray for physical healing in teams of two or more.
- Ask the person being prayed for what they want to ask God to do.
- Confirm that they are followers of Jesus. (If not, modify the prayer accordingly.)
- Ask whether or not they've prayed through freedom from generational bondage (page 53). If not, ask if they'd like to. If there's time, pray through this. If not, refer them to this for later prayer.
- Share with them that Christ became a curse for us and has the power to break every curse. See Gal 3:13 "Christ redeemed us from the curse of the law by becoming a curse for us—for it is written, 'Cursed is everyone who is hanged on a tree'". Ask if they would like God to break any curses affecting them, physical or otherwise, whether general or specific.
- Pray an opening prayer (page 8). Thank God for His overflowing love and goodness.
- If indicated, pray a simple prayer asking God to release them from generational bondage. Pray for release from anything related to their need for physical healing. Encourage them to soon pray more completely through generational bondage with a mature believer in Christ (page 53).
- If indicated, ask God to break any curses affecting them. Ask Him to bind and send away any evil powers involved in any way.
- Ask God to reveal to the person if there's anything in their lives or situation that's related in any way to their present physical condition. (This may include, but is not limited to, prayer burdens, sin to confess (page 99), someone to forgive (page 101), unresolved trauma (page 83), and emotional or spiritual stuck places.) Use Wholeness Prayer to pray through any issues God reveals. Listen to the Lord and follow His leading.

- Lay hands on them (as and when appropriate) and say, "Be healed, in the name of Jesus." Consider anointing them with oil (Mark 6:13, James 5:14). Pray further as God leads.
- Ask them how they're feeling, what they're sensing, and whether or not anything has changed in their physical condition. Pray and proceed further as God leads.
- Thank God for all He has done and ask Him to seal His victories and continue working, for His glory. Ask God to fill any empty places in them with Himself and protect them by His power. Pray blessing, joy and empowerment over them.
- Pray a closing prayer (page 12).
- Encourage them to follow Christ with all their hearts and continue to pray through any ways they feel stuck.
- If you were praying with a team, gather afterward. Pray for one another and rejoice in God's victories. If you were not praying with a team, you may find it helpful to ask another mature follower of Christ to pray with you.
- Rejoice over all He has done, is doing, and will do!

In addition to the above, if the person being prayed for is
- Not yet a follower of Christ, God may open doors through this experience to draw them to Himself. (See Chapter 31. Applications for Evangelism, page 205.)
- A first generation believer, freedom from generational bondage (page 53) may be especially important to address.
- Affected in a way that's similar to territorial spirits in the person's context, asking God to reveal that connection may give further insight for prayer. (See Chapter 34. Applications for Spiritual Warfare, page 223.)
- An intercessor, ask God to reveal if there are any ways in which their physical suffering is related to a prayer burden they have. Bind any related demonic elements in Jesus' name. Command them to go now where Jesus sends them and not return. Ask God to fully heal and protect the person. Ask Him to reveal how to pray into the situation. Follow through with any follow-up steps.

People who God heals physically (or in other ways) may experience this healing immediately or more gradually. If the healing is not immediate, those involved need discernment to know when a gradual healing is, in fact, in process. A gradual healing may take place over a long period of time, and involve multiple prayer times. It may also involve exercise, a change in habits, or other factors.

Gradual healings are quite common for those recovering from issues such as trauma, abuse, and addictions. Physical healings may also be gradual. If the healing is gradual, the person may be attacked by doubt and unbelief. They may have thoughts such as "Is anything really different?", "Am I making this up?", "If I tell someone, will it turn out later that nothing has really happened?" Doubt and unbelief are robbers. They attempt to steal spiritual victories. They might try to get us to stop persevering in prayer. Or they may rob our joy in the victories we've already experienced. Doubt and unbelief need to be recognized for what they are, and rebuked in Jesus' name.

Thanksgiving and gratitude are our appropriate responses. As we praise God for His love poured out over us, our spirits rejoice. He also speaks peace to our souls, and continues to heal us spiritually and emotionally.

Chapter 31. Applications for Evangelism

*For the Son of Man has come to seek
and to save that which was lost.*
~Luke 19:10 (NASB)

Nancy had recently lost her job. Her sister April, a new believer, listened compassionately to her story, then offered to pray for her. She used modified Wholeness Prayer principles and Jesus lifted Nancy's burden. Nancy then wanted to learn more about Jesus.

Using modified Wholeness Prayer principles with those who don't yet follow Christ can be very effective. Jesus delights to meet with those who are willing to come to Him. He cast demons out of people (Mark 5:1-20) and healed people (John 9:13-38) who did not yet believe that He was their Savior. He encourages all who are burdened to come to Him (Matthew 11:28-30). As people are healed and set free by His power, they often become more open to giving their lives to Him. They become more receptive to inviting Him to be their best friend forever.

When unbelievers confess their sins or are healed from their wounds, there may also be demonic forces present. You can command any demons, in the name of Jesus, to immediately leave, if they were present because of the sin or wound. However, if the person doesn't choose to receive Christ, they aren't guaranteed His protection. It's possible that demons could return and the person could end up worse off than before (Matthew 12:45). If the person does choose to receive Christ, they can ask Him to protect them and fill those empty places with Himself. In either case, returning to the sin can open people up to more bondage.

Wholeness Prayer can help with sharing the gospel.
- It breaks down barriers (e.g. fear, intimidation, anger, bitterness) in the lives of believers. This makes them better equipped to pray for people and spread the Good News: "...having shod [their] feet with the preparation of the gospel of peace" (Ephesians 6:15, NASB).
- It allows unbelievers to taste freedom from sin's effects and intimacy with God, available through Christ.

Keys that, at least in part, can be used with those who don't yet follow Christ
- Confessing and Turning from Sin (page 99)
- Breaking Internal Strongholds (page 129)
- Healing from Emotional Wounds (page 67)
- Praying through Trauma (page 83)
- Grieving Life's Losses (page 93)
- Forgiving Others (page 101)
- Forgiving One's Parents (page 107)
- Understanding God's Character (page 79)
- Replacing Counterfeit Desires (page 143)
- Developing Healthy Patterns (page 159).

Keys that would *not* be appropriate to use with those who don't yet follow Christ[82]
- Freedom from Generational Bondage (page 53)
- Replacing Family Curses with God's Blessings (page 75)
- Forgiving and Accepting Oneself (page 113)
- Breaking Unholy Covenants (page 123).

As you work with those who don't yet believe in Christ, ask God to help you know *when* and *how* to tell them more about Him. As God leads, let them know what other things they would be able to ask God for, if they were to choose to follow Him.

Chapter 32. Applications for Discipleship

You were taught, with regard to your former way of life,
to put off your old self,
which is being corrupted by its deceitful desires;
to be made new in the attitude of your minds;
and to put on the new self,
created to be like God in true righteousness and holiness.
~Ephesians 4:22-24 (NIV)

> "Sari was experiencing marriage and ministry problems due to bitterness she carried from childhood. Growing up in a missionary family she had experienced multiple difficulties, including financial struggles. As a teen, she had vowed not to be involved in ministry. Sari prayed through these issues with Lori, one of our Indonesian partners. Now she serves effectively among an unreached people group in Indonesia." ~L, Indonesia

Carl struggled with shame. He found it hard to believe that God could love him. As he prayed with Sam using Wholeness Prayer principles, Carl realized that his struggle was generational. God showed Carl how He would like to lift the burden of shame his father carries. Then Carl was able to receive God's acceptance and have his own burden of shame lifted. He chose to follow Jesus and his relationship with his wife improved.

Wholeness Prayer can radically advance our discipleship process as God's light ushers in His truth. Situations that trigger our pain can become doorways to greater freedom. Challenges and struggles in this life become opportunities for further growth. Old patterns lose their power to deceive, and we go forward with an increased capacity for holiness.

Wholeness Prayer principles can help you to increasingly grow in spiritual and emotional freedom. It can also help those with whom you're journeying together. You may want to ask other followers of Christ to help you pray through issues you struggle with. And others may find it helpful for you to pray with them.

If you think someone might benefit from Wholeness Prayer, here are a few things to keep in mind:
- You may or may not be the best person to help someone work through their issues at any given point in time.
- Issues that you think you see might not be actual issues. (You might have misinterpreted something, or be projecting your own issues onto them. Or you may have mixed motives or lack information. Your perspective could also be skewed by fear, insecurity, shame, hurt, anger or frustration.)
- Remember not to push, and always to *Follow Jesus*.

> "I struggled with ingrained sin patterns since 7th grade. It started with masturbation, then spread into compulsive overeating. I was weighed down with shame and guilt. Ten years later, through Wholeness Prayer, I finally gained victory over these sin patterns, and over much deeper issues.
>
> God used two main interweaving elements to begin and secure these victories: discipleship and healing through Wholeness Prayer. Throughout the time I struggled with these sin patterns, I shared with people dear to me, but there was no victory – no matter how we prayed. Part of the lack of victory was my inability to see God's truths that were eventually revealed in and through Wholeness Prayer. They were effectively birthed in my soul through the structure that Wholeness Prayer provides and the trust that was built through the discipleship process.
>
> Although I had prayed with many others about these sin patterns, it was the step-by-step process of recognize, recent, root, receive, renew (and rejoice!), the use of Wholeness Prayer keys, and the trust gained through meeting and communing weekly with my mentor that finally broke the barrier to hearing God's voice clearly.

This then opened the door to hearing God's truth on these sin patterns.

Through Wholeness Prayer and the steps involved in it, we were able to invite God into the midst of the problems in a very real way. The Wholeness Prayer method removed the chaos and the torment of the problems so that we could more easily address the issues. It opened many avenues through which God gave comfort and affirmation, and spoke truth. I received confirmation that what I was hearing really was from God, and that the healing He wanted to provide really was for me. When working through specific issues got tough, the structured pauses of Wholeness Prayer grounded whatever was going on and ushered in peace.

Working together with another person, especially a spiritually older mentor, was essential in helping me deal with these issues. This was because every time I encountered the issues, the pain was either too deep to bear alone with God, or I would turn to sinful escapes which compounded the issues with more confusion and torment.

A normal conversation with my mentor would have not brought the same solution that Wholeness Prayer did. The confusion brought on by sin had previously covered over the problems. The space we made for God through Wholeness Prayer, and the structure that was provided for Him to work, allowed Him to break the problems down into smaller digestible pieces, so the issues could be addressed. It brought up things from the past that I would have otherwise thought were irrelevant. If not for the support and affirmation that my mentor showed and my confidence in other people's testimonies of victories through Wholeness Prayer, I would not have gained the solutions that I did.

Through a Wholeness Prayer session with my mentor, God revealed to me that I'd felt very emotionally estranged from others throughout my life. As we prayed through different memories, I discovered God's healing and His desire to make me healed.

At first I was skeptical. I had a hard time trusting people. I'd spent years and years fighting addictions and dependencies, telling others about the issues, and waging war with my friends against these issues – all to no avail. I tried another version of healing prayer in order to break away from these addictions. While it was helpful to a great degree, many deep root issues remained concealed. Through Wholeness Prayer, the issues were able to be addressed. Over time, through Wholeness Prayer, my trust and connectedness with my mentor grew and my skepticism diminished. God eventually brought deliverance from the addictions and lack of emotional connection with others." ~C

If you'd like to use Wholeness Prayer principles with someone, but they haven't initiated
- Pray for the person, including any issues you think you might be observing.
- Ask God to open the door for you to pray with them in this way, if it's His will.
- Check that your motivation is love.
- Check that you are not trying to "fix" the person. God is the one who transforms us.
- Work through any similar issues in your own life.
- Share, as appropriate, how God has worked in your life as you've applied the principles in these modules.
- Look for some indication of interest on their part. Wait for this.
- Remember that God is the Healer.

Depending on your relationship with the person you think might benefit from Wholeness Prayer, you may also find some of the questions below useful. Following are important factors to keep in mind.
- The person may seem uncomfortable or reluctant to answer some of the questions you ask them. In such a case, you may not yet have a strong enough foundation of trust established to proceed at this level. Or there may be cultural or personality factors involved.
- Work to build trust as appropriate.
- Ask God for wisdom on how to proceed. *Follow Jesus.*
- As the person answers the questions you ask them,
  - Ask God to show you what things you might want to pursue together in prayer.
  - Pray through issues that arise as appropriate.
- Also consider answering these questions yourself. Your responses may help you see where Wholeness Prayer might be useful in your own life.

Questions you might find it useful to ask (yourself or others) when the person isn't aware of any specific issue they would like to pray through at present:
- What was life like for you growing up?
- What patterns did you see in your family, as you were growing up, that you would like to continue?
- What patterns would you not like to continue? Do you find yourself stuck in any of these?
- How is your communication with God?
- Are there areas where you struggle in your relationship with God?
- Are there areas where you struggle in your relationships with others (e.g. spouse, children, parents, colleagues, friends, opposite sex, same sex)?

Chapter 33. Applications for Conflict Resolution

If possible, so far as it depends on you, live peaceably with all.
~Romans 12:18 (ESV)

Put on then, as God's chosen ones, holy and beloved,
compassionate hearts, kindness, humility, meekness, and patience,
bearing with one another and,
if one has a complaint against another, forgiving each other;
as the Lord has forgiven you, so you also must forgive.
And above all these put on love,
which binds everything together in perfect harmony.
And let the peace of Christ rule in your hearts,
to which indeed you were called in one body.
And be thankful. Let the word of Christ dwell in you richly,
teaching and admonishing one another in all wisdom,
singing psalms and hymns and spiritual songs,
with thankfulness in your hearts to God.
And whatever you do, in word or deed,
do everything in the name of the Lord Jesus,
giving thanks to God the Father through him.
~Colossians 3:12-17 (ESV)

Ed, the leader of a large team, had a problem with insecurity and explosive anger. Tom and he brought this to God using Wholeness Prayer principles. Through this, Ed realized that his anger was being fed by shame, hurt and fear. He remembered a significant time in his childhood when he felt incompetent, hurt and alone. God spoke truth and peace into this memory and healed his wounds. Ed realized, for the first time, that God is with him and for him. God showed him a new pattern to apply in discipleship. Over time he grew in patience and resilience. The team he still leads grew in unity and a long-standing conflict was resolved.

1. **React or Respond?**

Oscar's father was frequently angry. Now when someone around Oscar starts to get angry, he freezes up and can't think how to handle it well. He just wants to escape or make them happy.

The most common reactions toward conflict are to attack or avoid. Both of these tend to be automatic reactions, rooted in our beliefs of what will help to keep us safe. The majority of people choose to avoid conflict.

A third choice is to pause, invite God in, and ask Him how to best respond. Many people are unaware of this third option, which includes hiding in God and seeking Him for wisdom on how to move forward.

The following questions can help you identify your response to conflict and why you choose to respond in these ways. Ask God to show you
- Whether or not you want to know when there's a conflict involving you (or those you lead)
- What you tend to do if you feel verbally threatened or attacked
- Whether or not you see conflict as an opportunity for growth.

Unhealthy patterns of addressing conflict include
- Not addressing issues in a timely manner or in a biblical fashion. Feeling offended and not addressing it quickly with the other person. Withdrawing from or not engaging in the conflict resolution process. Unforgiveness.
- Talking first with others not involved in the conflict and seeking their support or sympathy. Bringing others along to confront a person before going to them individually. Gossip. Not going to the other person about the problem because of feeling sure they won't listen.
- False assumptions, false accusations, suspicion. Assuming sin when the problem is really poor communication. Incorrect assumptions because of seeing through different lenses. Suspicion growing about motives, integrity and intent.

Other pitfalls may be encountered, such as
- Feeling attacked by the other party or by a mediator. Feeling one's reputation was hurt by the other party.
- Polarization of issues or groups. Factions.
- Low trust. Unmet needs for affirmation or appreciation.
- Anger. Resentment. Bitterness.
- Betrayal. Rejection.
- Fears.

When praying with someone who wants to learn to respond instead of react to conflict, you may find the following ideas helpful:
- If they would like to grow in navigating conflict in healthy ways, encourage them to tell God this and ask for His help.
- Ask God to show them anything within them that hinders them from addressing conflict in healthy ways. Use Wholeness Prayer to work through issues that emerge.
- Encourage them to identify and learn from healthy examples, and practice these new patterns.

2. Factors Involved in Conflict

The four most common types of conflict are[83]
- Miscommunication
- Differences – in culture, background, values, personality, opinion or preference
- Irresponsibility, lack of wisdom, or insensitivity to others' feelings
- Selfishness or other sins.

When conflict occurs, people often assume that whichever part of the conflict isn't their "fault" must be the other party's "fault." We often forget the role of spiritual warfare. And of other factors such as (but not limited to) miscommunication, differences in perspective, organizational dysfunction, or social pressures.

In addition to the current conflict, also of importance is the group's history of the conflict, and each person's personal history of this type of conflict.[84] Underlying fears are often a significant factor in conflict.[85]

Try taking a step back and asking God to reveal contributing factors in the conflict. This can greatly help increase perspective, decrease tensions, and address root issues. If possible, encourage all parties involved in the conflict to join together in prayer and worshipping God. Encourage them to thank Him for the things they do agree on and ask Him for breakthroughs. Also encourage them to ask Him to expose the role of spiritual warfare, and to totally crush all evil spirits involved. As they identify other external factors exacerbating the conflict, they can bring these to God as well.

3. Foundational Principles for Addressing Conflict

See God as infinitely bigger than any conflict.
- View conflicts from this perspective. Staying focused on Him and His bigness helps us to be hope bearers and move forward with confidence in His victory. This affects the tone of the interaction, giving it a God-focused resonance that leads upward.
- Recognize that conflicts are part of life and opportunities for Kingdom expansion (as in Acts 6:1-7).
- Understand that our true enemy is Satan, not one another (Ephesians 6:12).

Go to the cross and live in resurrection power.
- Plead with God to purify your own heart – including from things you're unaware of.
- Check your own attitude, especially in any areas you desire to address in another person.
- Be aware of how your own past experiences might influence your perspective.
- Repent of any sin, including any pride, gossip, or judgment.

- Ask God to show you anything you need to surrender (e.g. burdens, outcomes, idols, unholy desires). Give Him any desire you might have to look good, "save the day" or be a hero.
- Use Wholeness Prayer principles to work through your own issues. Ask others to help with this as seems wise.

Pray and worship a lot, with praise and thanksgiving – before, during and after the conflict resolution process. Praising and exalting God and proclaiming His glory is a powerful weapon of our warfare. It also helps us see more of God's bigness and gain perspective.
- Whenever possible, pray together *with* others involved. Seeking God's best together helps establish common ground.
- Use Scripture to fuel your prayers and shape your perspective.
- Rely on God. Ask Him to move in power to rout evil and break through in this situation, for His glory and the honor of His name.
  - Ask God to unmask the schemes of the evil one and totally defeat them.
  - Plead for unity, good communication, healthy relationships, speedy forgiveness, and wisdom regarding when and how much to trust the others involved.
  - Ask for God to get glory, and that His name not be dishonored. Ask that we would all exalt God in our words and through our actions.
  - Ask God to identify and break through any root issues, including hidden or unspoken ones.

Address spiritual dynamics.
- Ask God to move aside all powers and principalities involved, bind the evil one and loose the power of His Spirit. Consider the relevance of spiritual dynamics in the region and pray accordingly. Pray through your own generational bondage if you've not yet done this. Encourage others to do the same, if you're in a position to do so.
- Ask God to reveal ways in which evil feels threatened by those presently in conflict, if they were to work together in biblical love and unity. Moving ahead together in Christ they may be a serious threat to the kingdom of darkness.

- Ask God to reveal similarities in how each party feels offended by the other. These may be signs of underlying demonic interference.
- Ask God to reveal to all parties involved any factors exacerbating the conflict. Ask God (together if possible) to address these.

4. Helping Others Navigate Conflict Well

Each conflict between two people has three parts. The conflict itself, the history of similar past conflict between these people, and the history of any similar issues in each person involved.[86] If the conflict is between groups of people, then another layer of complexity is added.

A good first step when seeking to help others address conflict is to ask God (together whenever possible) to
- Move aside all powers and principalities involved in any way
- Bind and move aside all evil spirits involved in any way
- Pour out His Spirit over each person in the conflict, and over any mediators
- Move in power to bring forgiveness, reconciliation, restoration and healthy resolution to the issues.

Wholeness Prayer can help to identify and address the root issues involved in the conflict as we do the following:
- Talk with all involved, together when possible.
- Seek to identify the issues involved, with each party separately, and together when possible.
- Pray for resolution, together when possible.
- Encourage each person to pray through generational bondage (page 53), if they haven't already.
- Use Wholeness Prayer as needed to pray separately with each person (or group) and address issues that emerge.
- Meet together with both parties at once and see what progress can be made.
- Worship together and give thanks for what can be agreed upon.
- Repeat the process as needed.

In addition, we can seek to
- Help all involved to see the bigness of God, how much greater He is than the problem, and surrender all to Him. Encourage all involved to choose to totally depend on God and God alone – and speak and live from this perspective. He is our hope.
- Talk and pray with each party to help them identify issues to address in their own lives.
  - Gently (and often indirectly) help and encourage each person to look first at their own hearts and attitudes. Help them to become aware of how their past might influence their perspective, and to see their own sin. Pray and look for opportunities to address these. Sometimes it's best to not say anything. Ask God to move in power, and expectantly watch and wait – with patient urgency.
  - Encourage each person to identify and check out their underlying assumptions.
  - Notice when those involved don't seem to understand how others in the conflict might be feeling. Encourage them to consider this.
  - Encourage each person to ask God to help them know when they need to repent of something or grow in some way. And to know when they are being accused by evil forces and need to rebuke them.
- Recruit those involved to pray and worship.

When praying with someone who wants to grow in helping others navigate conflict well, you may find the following ideas helpful:
- Encourage them to tell God that they would like to grow in helping others navigate conflict, and ask for His help.
- Use Wholeness Prayer to work through any issues that emerge in them. Encourage them to keep this in mind as they work through the ideas in this chapter.
- Ask God to help them be aware of their attitude toward conflict.
- Ask God to help them grow in their sensitivity and awareness of brewing conflicts. And to address these early on, before they escalate.

- Ask God to help them be aware of their attitude toward the specific issues within a conflict. And how this might help or hinder their ability to assist in resolving the conflict.
- Encourage them to grow in understanding the four most common causes of conflicts and how to address them.
- Ask God to help them stay focused on Him and His bigness.

5. Applications for Married Couples

A married couple may ask you for help with their relationship. When possible first meet with both the husband and the wife together. (In some cases, you will only be able to meet with one of them.) With God's help, seek to identify, together with them

- Unhealthy patterns in their relationship
- Generational bondage
- Unhealed wounds, unconfessed sin or unforgiveness
- Ongoing stressors or conflicts
- Other things He wants to address.

Encourage each spouse to use Wholeness Prayer to pray through any issues that arise. They can do this on their own or with your help (or someone else's) as desired. As issues are addressed, encourage the couple to work through appropriate follow-up steps. Prioritize those relating to how they communicate with each other. Meet with both of them as appropriate. Remember that you are partnering with God and that He is the Great Counselor.

6. Resources

- "Living in the Path of Peace"
  <http://ent.freemin.org/conflict-management/>
- "Wise Doves and Innocent Serpents: Doing Conflict Resolution Better"
  <http://mcaresources.googlepages.com/realitydose>
  by Dr. Kelly O'Donnell (accessed May 27, 2017)
- *The Relationship Cure: A 5 Step Guide to Strengthening Your Marriage, Family, and Friendships* by John Gottman
- *Counseling Couples in Conflict: A Relational Restoration Model* by James N. Sells and Mark A. Yarhouse
- *The Marriage Builder: Creating True Oneness to Transform Your Marriage* by Larry Crabb

Chapter 34. Applications for Spiritual Warfare

If God is for us, who can be against us?
~Romans 8:31b (NIV)

Finally, be strong in the Lord and in the strength of His might. Put on the full armor of God, so that you will be able to stand firm against the schemes of the devil. For our struggle is not against flesh and blood, but against the rulers,
against the powers, against the world forces of this darkness, against the spiritual forces of wickedness in the heavenly place.
~Ephesians 6:10 (NASB)

Spiritual warfare abounds in our world, affecting a variety of contexts. These include individuals, relationships, groups, leaders, and the spiritual realm. Whatever the spiritual warfare situation may be, we are empowered by God to overcome as we

- *Follow Jesus*
- *Recognize* the warfare and its *recent* effects
- Seek to identify the *root*
- Ask God to pour out His power to address the root and help the context (whatever it may be) to *receive* His Kingdom opposites and be *renew*ed for His glory
- Follow through with any action steps, including persevering in prayer to complete victory.

A significant aspect of spiritual warfare is tearing down strongholds in Jesus' mighty name. These are things that set themselves up against the knowledge of Christ. Strongholds differ from one context to another. They have increased layers of complexity when occult bondage (page 59) is involved.

We've looked at using Wholeness Prayer to address strongholds in individual lives and relationships. Territorial strongholds also affect communities, peoples and nations.

If we feel spiritual oppression, we often assume the cause is something within ourselves. But it may also be external, related to a situation, group, or area. These external forces may try to insert thoughts into our heads, intimidate us, or cause us to become irritated. Or they may seek to trick us in some other way.

1. **When addressing spiritual oppression in a situation, group, or area**, you may find the following steps helpful:
   - Ask God to help you be quick to recognize any type of spiritual oppression.
   - Ask God to show you any spiritual warfare dynamics you might be overlooking in a situation.
   - When you sense some type of oppression, ask God for discernment. Seek to know whether the *root* is internal, external or a mixture. To help sort this out,
     - Command any external oppressive forces to be bound and silenced in the name of Jesus. Tell them to go where Jesus sends them, and to not oppress you anymore.
     - Then see what remains. In God's timing, work through any internal issues, using Wholeness Prayer.
   - Ask God for discernment in addressing any external forces that have been identified.

In seeking to address territorial strongholds in prayer, *following Jesus* is paramount. It's His name and His blood that overcomes. The 5 R's can help empower our prayers, as we ask God to
- Help us *recognize* strongholds in a place, area, or people group
- Help us identify the *recent* effects of territorial strongholds in individual lives, relationships, and communities
- Show us what we need to know about the *root* of the problem. Help us find relevant Bible verses. Give us insight into how to pray, including extraordinary prayer strategies.[87]
- *Reveal* Himself powerfully in each situation and context, and to those within the context
- *Renew* each situation, context and person with His Kingdom opposites. Tear down strongholds in His name (e.g. faithfulness instead of adultery, hope instead of despair, truth instead of lies, honor instead of disgrace).

2. The Weapons of Our Warfare

> *For though we walk in the flesh,*
> *we do not war according to the flesh,*
> *for the weapons of our warfare are not of the flesh,*
> *but divinely powerful for the destruction of fortresses.*
> ~2 Corinthians 10:3-4 (NASB)

J.F.K. Mensah explains, "We must believe in the weapons of our warfare. If we have a hammer and we hit the rock once with the hammer, then throw the hammer away because the rock didn't break yet, we aren't believing in the weapon. Over time there is no curse that can't be broken. To believe otherwise is to believe a lie. Have courage! You are seated with Christ in heavenly places. You are tiny, but the weapons are mighty."[88]

We're actively involved in a spiritual battle, whether or not we choose to be. We can only choose which side we're on – the Kingdom of God or the kingdom of this world. We've been raised up with Christ and are seated with Him (Ephesians 2:4-7). This is a place of victory.

Walter Wink writes, "Intercessors have an essential role to play in creating a better future for our world, because intercession is spiritual defiance of what is in the name of what God has promised. The shape of the future will be determined by those who can survey all its various possibilities and who, by faith, latch on to one as inevitable. History belongs to the intercessors who thus believe the future into being."[89]

As the fields of our lives are restored and bear fruit, we get back what has been robbed from us. We get in position to more powerfully join in the cry for His Kingdom to come and His will to be done. All over the earth, as it is in Heaven (Matthew 6:9-10).

Epilogue. Where Will You Go from Here?

1. Questions for Reflection
- What are your goals for using Wholeness Prayer? What will help you reach those goals?
- How do you want to apply the 5 R's, and in what contexts?
- What concrete action steps do you choose to pursue? When do you plan to do them?
- Is it worth the effort it will take? Can you do it, with God helping you?
- Who will you ask to help you reach these goals? When do you plan to ask them?

2. My Prayer

The Lord bless you and keep you;
the Lord make his face shine on you and be gracious to you;
the Lord turn his face toward you and give you peace.
~Numbers 6:24-26 (NIV)

Appendix 1. Facilitating a Time of Wholeness Prayer

Basic Principles

- **Claim your heritage** – Reclaim it if you've been robbed. 1 Peter 1:3-9
- **Come to Jesus** – Bring Him your stuck places. Psalm 62:5-8
- **3-way prayer** – The facilitator does most of the verbal prayer. The person being prayed for focuses on listening to God and responding. Others intercede quietly. Matthew 18:18-20
- **Hearing God** – God speaks directly to the person being prayed for at their point of need. Spend time silently listening for His voice. John 10:27
- **Test and give thanks** – Give thanks frequently during the prayer time. Test to confirm that all the person hears is consistent with Scripture. 1 Thessalonians 5:16-21
- **Follow Jesus** above all. Let Him lead the process. John 8:12, 31-32
- **Confidentiality** – Share only your own story, not someone else's. Romans 1:28-32, Proverbs 20:19

5 R's + Opening Prayer and Closing Prayer

- **Opening Prayer** – Ask God to lead and protect. Bind evil in Jesus' name. Matthew 18:18-20, Psalm 143:10, Proverbs 18:10

- **Recognize** – Identify (take captive) negative feelings, thoughts, and actions. 2 Corinthians 10:3-5
  - Ask God to show the person being prayed for
    - Where they struggle (with negative feelings, thoughts, or actions)
    - Which of their struggles He would like to talk to them about today.
  - Intercede silently as the person listens for God's voice. After a minute or so, ask them to share with you (as much as they desire) what God's showing them.

- **Recent** – Bring these struggles to God and ask Him to reveal a related recent memory. 2 Corinthians 10:5
  - Thank God for what He has revealed, then ask Him to show the person being prayed for
    - A recent time this (feeling, thought, or action) occurred
    - How they felt
    - What they believed at a heart level.
  - Intercede silently as the person listens for God's voice. After a minute or so, ask them to share with you (as much as they desire) what God's showing them.

- **Root** – Ask God to reveal any root(s) – the first time (or pattern) when the person being prayed for thought, felt, and/or acted this way. Matthew 12:33
  - Thank God for what He has revealed. Then ask Him to help the person being prayed for to connect with this recent memory and the related feelings and beliefs. As they do, ask God to show them
    - The first time this (feeling, thought, or action) occurred in their life (or if it has been a pattern)
    - How they felt
    - What they believed at a heart level.
  - Intercede silently as the person listens for God's voice. After a minute or so, ask them to share with you (as much as they desire) what God's showing them.

- **Receive** – Receive His perspective - first at the root, if there is one. Test by God's Word. Matthew 7:7-11
  - Thank God for what He has revealed. Then ask God to show the person being prayed for whether or not they would like to invite Him into this memory (or pattern).
    - If they would like to, encourage them to do so.
    - If not, but they would still like to pursue the process, ask God to show them why not. Use the 5 R's to work through those reasons before returning to this step.
  - Ask God to help the person being prayed for to connect with this root memory (or pattern) and the related feelings and beliefs. As they do, ask God to reveal in the root memory (or pattern)
    - His perspective
    - Any ways He wants them to respond (e.g. forgive someone)

- Anything that does not yet feel peaceful.
  - Intercede silently as the person listens for God's voice. After a minute or so, ask them to share with you (as much as they desire of) what God's showing them.
  - Encourage them to pray aloud when making any decisions. These might include forgiving someone or making requests (e.g. breaking unhealthy emotional bonds).
  - Test what they are hearing by God's Word. If anything they're hearing is not consistent with God's Word, pray through this inconsistency using the 5 R's.
  - Thank God for the things He's revealing.
  - Continue to pray through the root memory (or pattern) until it is filled with peace.

- **Renew** – Apply this perspective in everyday life. 1 John 1:5-7
  - Thank God for what He has revealed, then ask God to show the person being prayed for
    - How this same truth applies in the recent memory
    - How this same truth applies to similar situations in the future
    - Any follow-up steps to pursue.
  - Intercede silently as the person being prayed for listens for God's voice. After a minute or so, ask them to share with you (as much as they desire) what God's showing them.
  - Test what they are hearing by God's Word. If anything they're hearing is not consistent with God's Word, pray through this inconsistency using the 5 R's.
  - Thank God for the things He's revealing.

- **Closing Prayer** – Thank God and ask for help to apply His truth. Send away evil in Jesus' name. Luke 17:11-19, John 8:31, Luke 10:17-19

Notes:

- *If the person being prayed for gets stuck anywhere in this process, ask God to reveal why. If they're still stuck, pray a closing prayer of protection. Then, with the person's permission, ask your mentor for help. If you don't have a mentor, refer the person to someone who can better help them.*

- *If there's not time to finish the Wholeness Prayer process in one setting, pray a closing prayer of protection. Ask God to continue the healing process. The next time you meet for Wholeness Prayer, ask God to show the person being prayed for where they are in the process. And what is on God's heart and the person's heart to pray through next.*

Appendix 2. Other Freedom for the Captives Resources

Commonly used in and together with Wholeness Prayer
Available on www.freemin.org

- Simplified Version of Wholeness Prayer
  <http://ent.freemin.org/simplified-version/>
  – the booklet currently used in trainings around the world and available in multiple languages. Including basic principles and commonly used keys, it's a useful reference when praying with someone.
- Discovery Bible Studies
  <http://ent.freemin.org/discovery-bible-studies/>
  – to use with a group learning Wholeness Prayer Principles together.
- Wholeness Prayer Small Group Guide
  <http://ent.freemin.org/simplified-version/>
  – a one-page guide for use by groups learning to pray with one another using Wholeness Prayer.
- Growing in Hearing God
  <http://ent.freemin.org/hearing-god/>
  – useful when intentionally pursuing hearing God more, identifying hindrances, and overcoming them.
- Connecting with Feelings
  <http://en.freemin.org/connecting-with-feelings/>
  – practical ideas for growing in connecting with feelings.
- Conflict Management
  <http://en.freemin.org/conflict-management/>
  – Living in the Path of Peace – a four-part guide with insights for identifying and navigating conflicts.

Appendix 3. Keys Used in W[...] Prayer

Basic Principle: Follow Jesus

Opening Prayer
- Invite God to lead the prayer time. Ask Him to accomp[lish what] He desires through it.
- Ask for His protection. Bind the evil one and forbid him t[o] interfere, in Jesus' name.

5 R's
- Recognize
- Recent
- Root
- Receive
- Renew

Freedom from Generational Bondage
- Identify generational bondage at work in their family of origin.
- They confess this and ask God to protect them.
- Work through any follow-up steps.

Freedom from Occult Bondage
- Identify, confess and repent of occult involvement.
- Pray through related issues.
- Break the power of occult bondage in the person's life.
- Ask God to shut every door to evil in the person's life.
- Ask God to fill every part of the person with Christ.
- Destroy occult objects.
- Ask God to protect the person and their family.

Emotional Wounds based on False Beliefs
Identify
- Feelings
- False beliefs
- Root memory (or pattern)

...on Truth
...iah 53:4).

...on.
...(underlying) emotion – often frustration, ...hurt.

...with Blessings
...ngs.
...ses with blessings.
...ings.

...anding God's Character
...tify misperceptions of God's character.
...parate who God truly is from unhealthy role models.

Praying through Trauma
- Work through each event in the trauma.
- Ask God to carry the burden of the trauma.
- Bind and cast out any evil spirits connected to the trauma.

Praying through Abuse
- The person being prayed for invites God to speak to the root memory or pattern.

Grieving Life's Losses
- Working through grief and loss is a process.
- People can get stuck in the grieving process. If this happens, it can be worked through.
- God wants to walk alongside those who grieve and carry their unpleasant emotions (Isaiah 53:4).

Confessing and Turning from Sin
- Pray through anything that contributed to the decision to sin in this way (why they chose it).

Forgiving Others
- Bind and cast out evil spirits related to the offenses.
- Forgive the person and fully release the offenses to God.
- Receive and bless the person being forgiven.

Forgiving One's Parents
- Objectively separate their parent from their parent's sins and weaknesses.
- Take responsibility for their own actions.
- Focus on Jesus and follow Him.
- Accept and bless their parent.
- Forgive their parent's sin.

Forgiving Oneself
- Identify why forgiving themselves is hard.
- Pray through related issues.
- Receive grace and forgiveness.
- Extend grace and forgiveness.

Accepting Oneself
- Identify why accepting themselves is hard.
- Pray through related issues.
- Receive God's acceptance.
- Extend acceptance to themselves.

Developing Healthy Boundaries
- Find healthy boundaries.
- Apply healthy boundaries.

Breaking Unholy Covenants
- Identify unholy covenants.
- Confess and turn from unholy covenants.
- Break the power of unholy covenants.
- Ask God to fill the person with Himself and protect them by His power.

Breaking Unholy One-Flesh Bonds
- Pray through anything that contributed to a decision to sin in this way (if their decision played a role in it).
- Break, restore, cleanse.
- Develop healthy boundaries.

Breaking Internal Strongholds
- Identify internal strongholds and why these were chosen.
- Work through related issues.
- Ask God to break the power of internal strongholds, fill the person with Himself and protect them by His power.

  1. **Unwise Decisions**
     - Identify unwise decisions and why these were chosen.
     - Work through related issues.
     - Replace false beliefs with truth.

  2. **Unhealthy Vows**
     - Identify unwise and negative vows and why these were chosen.
     - Work through related issues.
     - Ask God to nullify unwise and negative vows.

  3. **Negative Scripts**
     - Identify old scripts.
     - Choose to accept, reject or modify these.
     - Ask God for His help to walk in new patterns.

  4. **Cursing Others**
     - Identify ways in which the person has cursed others and why they did this.
     - Work through related issues.
     - Ask God to break the power of the curses and replace them with blessings.

  5. **Feeling Cursed**
     - Work through root and related issues.
     - Ask God to break the power of any curses and replace them with a blessing.
     - Ask God to protect the person.

6. **Feeling Judged**
   - Identify ways the person has felt judged.
   - Work through root issues.
   - Ask God to break the power of the judgment and replace it with a blessing.

7. **Judging Others**
   - Identify ways in which the person has judged others and why they chose to do so.
   - Work through root issues.
   - Ask God to break the power of the judgment and replace it with a blessing.

8. **Unhealthy Emotional Bonds**
   - Identify unhealthy emotional bonds and why they were chosen.
   - Work through root issues.
   - Ask God to *break* unhealthy bonds and *replace* them with healthy bonds.
   - Find and apply healthy boundaries.

Replacing Counterfeit Desires
- Identify counterfeit desires.
- Work through related issues.
- Replace counterfeit desires with underlying true desires.

Overcoming Unhealthy Fear
- Work through root issues.
- Rebuke unhealthy fear in Jesus' name.
- Ask God to fill the person with Himself and protect them by His power.

1. **Replacing Fear Bonds with Love Bonds**
   - Identify fear bonds.
   - Work through root issues.
   - Break fear bonds and replace with love bonds.
   - Develop healthy boundaries.

2. **Overcoming Panic Attacks**
   - Work through related issues.
   - Bind and rebuke unhealthy fear.
   - Ask God to protect the person and fill them with Himself.

3. **No Longer a Victim**
   - Know who they are in Christ.
   - Know their authority in Christ.
   - Know that they are protected and empowered by God.
   - Work through related issues.

Finding True Security
- Identify roots of insecurity.
- Work through related issues.
- Grow in knowing who God is.

Developing Healthy Patterns
- Identify the unhealthy pattern.
- Find the root (the first unpleasant emotion in the cycle and what triggered it).
- Find the healthy way back to joy from initial unpleasant emotion.
- Ask God how to respond to the initial situation in a healthy way.
- Understand and apply a new, healthy pattern.

   1. **Escaping a Looping Bowtie Pattern**
      - Identify their own unhealthy contribution to the pattern.
      - Work through related issues.
      - Learn to respond in a healthy way.

   2. **Freedom from the Drama Triangle**
      - Identify unhealthy patterns of relating as victim, rescuer, or persecutor.
      - Pray through root issues.
      - Pray the power of the Trinity over the drama triangle – to break unhealthy relational patterns and replace them with healthy patterns.
      - Learn and apply healthy patterns.

3. **Applications for Obsessive-Compulsive Behavior**
   - Reframe the problem: The real issue is with the thought patterns.
   - Refocus the thoughts.

Giving Up Unhealthy Control
- Surrender outcomes to God.
- Seek related Bible verses and promises. Use these to pray into the situation.
- Follow through with any action steps God reveals.

Overcoming Perfectionism
- Unmask perfectionism.
- Work through underlying issues.

Overcoming Addictions
- Identify related root emotions, family patterns, social pressure and/or longing for connection.
- Identify addictive roots, cloaks, patterns and mindsets, and invite God in.
- Process, practice and pray through with God until total victory is reached.

1. **Overcoming Eating Disorders**
   - Identify root issues and triggers.
   - Work through related issues.
   - Persevere.

Addressing Unhealthy Relationship Styles
- Identify unhealthy relationship styles and patterns.
- Work through root issues.
- Grow toward relating in healthy ways with God, oneself and others.

Closing Prayer
- Thank God for all He's done during the prayer time.
- Ask Him to help the person apply His truth in their daily lives.
- Command any evil spirits connected with the issues that have been prayed through, in the name of Jesus, to go wherever Jesus sends them and never return.
- Ask God to protect all involved.
- Ask God to fill any empty places in the person with Himself.
- Ask God to remind the person of the new path He has revealed each time they encounter a similar situation.
- Ask God to help them consistently choose this new path.

Follow up
- Ask the person if there's anything else they'd like to share with you about what God did during the prayer time.
- Encourage them to
    - Share, with others whom they trust, what God has done
    - Meditate on related Scriptures
    - Follow through with any follow-up steps God has shown them
    - Continue to thank God for His victories.

Appendix 4. Biblical Foundations of Wholeness

"In the Bible, shalom means universal flourishing, wholeness and delight — a rich state of affairs in which natural needs are satisfied and natural gifts fruitfully employed, a state of affairs that inspires joyful wonder as its Creator and Savior opens doors and welcomes the creatures in whom He delights."[90]

Old Testament Concept of Peace

"...shalom is a very flexible word and can refer to much more than peace as merely freedom from strife and disorder; harmony; and to be quiet.' Yet, all of the many meanings of shalom, including friendship, well-being, safety and salvation - clearly reflect various aspects of 'completeness,' the fundamental meaning of the Hebrew root SH-L-M."[91]

"The Lord bless you and keep you; the Lord make his face shine on you and be gracious to you; the Lord turn his face toward you and give you peace [shalom]" (Numbers 6:24-26, NIV).

"The Lord sat as King at the flood; Yes, the Lord sits as King forever. The Lord will give strength to His people; The Lord will bless His people with peace [shalom]" (Psalm 29:10-11, NASB).

"How blessed is the man who finds wisdom And the man who gains understanding.... Her ways are pleasant ways And all her paths are peace [shalom]" (Proverbs 3:13 and 17, NASB).

"For a child will be born to us, a son will be given to us; And the government will rest on His shoulders; And His name will be called Wonderful Counselor, Mighty God, Eternal Father, Prince of Peace [shalom]. There will be no end to the increase of His government or of peace [shalom]" (Isaiah 9:6-7a, NASB).

"The steadfast of mind You will keep in perfect peace [shalom], Because he trusts in You" (Isaiah 26:3, NASB).

New Testament Concept of Peace

"In classic Greek, peace is the state of law and order that gives rise to the blessing of prosperity. It is also used to denote peaceful conduct toward others. The New Testament use of eiréné remains firmly based in the Hebrew traditions of shalom in the Tenach. It can describe both the content and the goal of all Christian preaching, since the message is called the Gospel of Peace (Ephesians 6:15)."[92]

"Peace [eiréné] I leave with you; my peace I give you. I do not give to you as the world gives. Do not let your hearts be troubled and do not be afraid" (John 14:27, NIV).

"I have told you these things, so that in me you may have peace [eiréné]. In this world you will have trouble. But take heart! I have overcome the world" (John 16:33, NASB).

"You know the message God sent to the people of Israel, announcing the good news of peace [eiréné] through Jesus Christ, who is Lord of all" (Acts 10:36, NIV).

"May the God of hope fill you with all joy and peace [eiréné] as you trust in him, so that you may overflow with hope by the power of the Holy Spirit" (Romans 15:13, NIV).

"But the fruit of the Spirit is love, joy, peace [eiréné], forbearance, kindness, goodness, faithfulness, gentleness and self-control. Against such things there is no law" (Galatians 5:22-23, NIV).

"Rejoice in the Lord always. I will say it again: Rejoice! Let your gentleness be evident to all. The Lord is near. Do not be anxious about anything, but in every situation, by prayer and petition, with thanksgiving, present your requests to God. And the peace [eiréné] of God, which transcends all understanding, will guard your hearts and your minds in Christ Jesus. Finally, brothers and sisters, whatever is true, whatever is noble, whatever is right, whatever is pure, whatever is lovely, whatever is admirable—if anything is excellent or praiseworthy—think about such things. Whatever you have learned or received or heard from me, or seen in me—put it into practice. And the God of peace [eiréné] will be with you" (Philippians 4:4-9, NIV).

"Now may the Lord of peace [eiréné] himself give you peace at all times and in every way. The Lord be with all of you" (2 Thessalonians 3:16, NIV).

"Grace, mercy and peace [eiréné] from God the Father and from Jesus Christ, the Father's Son, will be with us in truth and love" (2 John 1:3, NIV).

Key Concepts

1. People were created to live in shalom.
God saw all that he had made, and it was very good (Genesis 1:31a, NIV).

2. Humanity chose to follow our own ways instead.
The man said, "The woman you put here with me—she gave me some fruit from the tree, and I ate it." Then the Lord God said to the woman, "What is this you have done?" The woman said, "The serpent deceived me, and I ate" (Genesis 3:12-13, NIV).

3. God made a way for us to be rescued.
Surely he took up our pain and bore our suffering, yet we considered him punished by God, stricken by him, and afflicted. But he was pierced for our transgressions, he was crushed for our iniquities; the punishment that brought us peace [shalom] *was on him, and by his wounds we are healed* (Isaiah 53:4-5, NIV).

4. Superficial/counterfeit peace is not enough.
Because they lead my people astray, saying, "Peace [shalom]*," when there is no peace* [shalom] *and because, when a flimsy wall is built, they cover it with whitewash, therefore tell those who cover it with whitewash that it is going to fall. Rain will come in torrents, and I will send hailstones hurtling down, and violent winds will burst forth. When the wall collapses, will people not ask you,*

"Where is the whitewash you covered it with?" (Ezekiel 13:10-12, NIV).

5. We are to seek to live in peace with one another.
Finally, brothers and sisters, rejoice! Strive for full restoration, encourage one another, be of one mind, live in peace [eiréné]. *And the God of love and peace* [eiréné] *will be with you* (2 Corinthians 13:11, NIV).

6. We are being transformed.
I pray that the eyes of your heart may be enlightened in order that you may know the hope to which he has called you, the riches of his glorious inheritance in his holy people, and his incomparably great power for us who believe. That power is the same as the mighty strength he exerted when he raised Christ from the dead and seated him at his right hand in the heavenly realms, far above all rule and authority, power and dominion, and every name that is invoked, not only in the present age but also in the one to come (Ephesians 1:18-21, NIV).

7. Someday all creation will be made completely new and whole; shalom will be fully realized.
Dear friends, now we are children of God, and what we will be has not yet been made known. But we know that when Christ appears, we shall be like him, for we shall see him as he is. (1 John 3:2, NIV).

Then I saw "a new heaven and a new earth," for the first heaven and the first earth had passed away, and there was no longer any sea. I saw the Holy City, the new Jerusalem, coming down out of heaven from God, prepared as a bride beautifully dressed for her husband. And I heard a loud voice from the throne saying, "Look! God's dwelling place is now among the people, and he will dwell with them. They will be his people, and God himself will be with them and be their God. 'He will wipe every tear from their eyes. There will be no more death' or mourning or crying or pain, for the old order of things has passed away" (Revelation 21:1-4, NIV).

Endnotes

[1] USA, Indonesia, India, Canada, Brazil, Peru, England, Turkey, the Czech Republic, Germany, Egypt, New Zealand, Australia, Ghana, and Uganda.

[2] God may reveal something directly to the person, or He may simply help them to (1) remember something that happened, (2) identify their thoughts and feelings, or (3) connect emotionally with truths they already are familiar with at a cognitive level. He created us and comes alongside us to help us process our thoughts and emotions, and find His peace. What God's revealing and what the person being prayed for is simply remembering or connecting with at a deeper level are often intertwined.

Wholeness Prayer is built on the sufficiency of Scripture as the only infallible way of knowing the will and truth of God. All thoughts, feelings and impressions must be tested according to the inerrant standard of biblical truth. When we ask God to "reveal" something, we are not asking for a new revelation in the sense of an inerrant new message such as is found in the Bible. We are asking Him, by His Spirit, to bring to mind biblical truth. We ask Him to illuminate and apply that truth, and to bring to light realities within a person's experience and inner life, so that His (biblical) truth can be applied to those realities.

[3] Occasionally this memory will be a dream the person recently had, or a recurring dream.

[4] If the root of the problem is false teaching only, and doesn't involve an emotional wound, the person may need help to understand the truth of Scripture. You may or may not be the best person to help them with this. If you aren't, refer them to someone who listens well and is able to clearly and compassionately explain spiritual truths. If you are helping them to process theological truths, first clarify that this is not part of the Wholeness Prayer process.

[5] NIV

[6] NIV

[7] ESV

[8] Examples include a sense of oppression, an inability to read Scripture, multiple distractions, ongoing confusion or distortions.

[9] In this type of context, Wholeness Prayer offers the benefit of not needing to know more than the general outline of a situation to bring it before God. God is the Great Counselor, and He already knows the details of the issues involved.

[10] NASB

[11] "Dissociation is a mental process that causes a lack of connection in a person's thoughts, memory and sense of identity. ... A severe and more chronic form of dissociation is seen in the disorder Dissociative Identity Disorder, once called Multiple Personality Disorder, and other Dissociative Disorders." www.mentalhealthamerica.net/conditions/dissociation-and-dissociative-disorders, accessed March 14, 2017

[12] This is further explained in the section regarding finding the Root, Chapter 2, page 10.

[13] Adapted with permission from *A Theory and Process for Christian Counseling & Inner Healing* by Alfred C.W. Davis, MBA, M.Div., pages 31-33.
[14] ibid, pages 33-34. This list is not meant to be fully comprehensive.
[15] ibid, page 139-140
[16] "What Is the Occult?" ChristianAnswers.net. http://www.christiananswers.net/q-eden/edn-occult-defn.html, accessed March 14, 2017.
[17] Many of the items on this list, and more, are listed on the above webpage.
[18] *Undivided Heart Prayer Ministry* by Anna Travis, pages 16-17.
[19] Adapted with permission from ibid, pages 17-18.
[20] Adapted with permission from *A Theory and Process for Christian Counseling & Inner Healing*, pages 155-156.
[21] Matthew 22:37 (NIV)
[22] Adapted with permission from *Undivided Heart Prayer Ministry*, pages 18-19.
[23] If you are praying with someone and these issues emerge, it may be best to refer the person to someone with more experience helping people pray through these types of issues. Before beginning a Wholeness Prayer session, remember to clarify if you are not certified as a counselor.
[24] Adapted with permission from *A Theory and Process for Christian Counseling & Inner Healing*, pages 45-50, 143-149. Similar concepts can also be found in *"Beyond Tolerable Recovery"* by Ed M. Smith.
[25] For examples of negative emotions, see Connecting with Feelings <http://ent.freemin.org/connecting-with-feelings/>.
[26] Some people feel that because of their situation during childhood, they lost the opportunity to "just be a child."
[27] Kim Pratt, LCSV, Psychology Tools: "What is Anger? A Secondary Emotion," published February 3, 2014, https://healthypsych.com/psychology-tools-what-is-anger-a-secondary-emotion/, accessed March 14, 2017.
[28] Adapted with permission from *A Theory and Process for Christian Counseling & Inner Healing*, pages 35-37.
[29] While occult cursing is a possibility, more commonly this refers to hurtful words that impacted a child's identity.
[30] "Post-traumatic stress disorder (PTSD) is an anxiety disorder caused by very stressful, frightening or distressing events. Someone with PTSD often relives the traumatic event through nightmares and flashbacks, and may experience feelings of isolation, irritability and guilt. They may also have problems sleeping, such as insomnia, and find concentrating difficult. These symptoms are often severe and persistent enough to have a significant impact on the person's day-to-day life." NCH Choices, http://www.nhs.uk/conditions/post-traumatic-stress-disorder/pages/introduction.aspx, accessed March 14, 2017.
[31] Definition from *Funk & Wagnalls Standard College Dictionary*, copyright © 1977 by Harper & Row, Publishers, Inc.

[32] If the person has experienced multiple traumas over their lifetime, it may help to ask God to carry the burden of all the traumas combined. Also to bind and cast out any evil spirits connected to all the traumas combined. Then ask God to bring key traumas to the person's mind, beginning with the earliest one. As He does, pray through each one as described in this chapter. Continue until all feels peaceful to the person being prayed for. This may involve multiple prayer sessions.

[33] These stages are a variation of the five stages of grief "first proposed by Elisabeth Kübler-Ross in her 1969 book *On Death and Dying*." Julie Axelrod, "The 5 Stages of Grief & Loss," https://psychcentral.com/lib/the-5-stages-of-loss-and-grief/, accessed March 14, 2017.

[34] The Bargaining Stage of Grief, by Alexis Aiger, Last Updated: Nov 18, 2015, www.livestrong.com/article/143100-the-bargaining-stage-grief/, accessed March 14, 2017.

[35] For example Psalm 55, 64, 69, 70.

[36] Concept from *The Speed of Trust* and *Smart Trust*, both by Stephen M. Covey. "Smart Trust analysis involves the assessment of 3 vital variables: 1. Opportunity (the situation – what you're trusting someone with); 2. Risk (the level of risk involved); 3. Credibility (the character and competence of the people involved)... The objective of Smart Trust is to manage risk wisely – to extend trust in a way that will maximize prosperity, energy and joy." *Smart Trust*, page 60.

[37] *Breaking the Bonds of Our Past* by Douglas Hayward, PhD., page 16.

[38] Adapted with permission from *A Theory and Process for Christian Counseling & Inner Healing*, pages 107-122, 164 and 165.

[39] Those who don't yet follow Christ aren't yet forgiven by Him. See Chapter 31. Applications for Evangelism, page 205.

[40] Those who don't yet follow Christ aren't yet accepted by Him. See Chapter 31. Applications for Evangelism, page 205.

[41] You may want to share some verses with the person being prayed for after the prayer time. Examples include Ephesians 1-3.

[42] Adapted with permission from *A Theory and Process for Christian Counseling & Inner Healing*, pages 139-140.

[43] They may already be aware of verses that address the issue. They might also do a word search on a website such as www.biblegateway.com. Or they might ask other followers of Jesus what verses they've found helpful. (Verses are also included with each type of stronghold being discussed. See page 131ff.)

[44] *Funk & Wagnalls Standard College Dictionary,* copyright © 1977 by Harper & Row, Publishers, Inc.

[45] Concept from a private conversation with Dr. David Wickstrom in March, 2003.

[46] Adapted with permission from *Undivided Heart Prayer Ministry* by Anna Travis, page 13.

[47] ibid

[48] Ibid

[49] The word fear, as often used in this book, refers to unhealthy fear. There is also healthy fear. In *The Practice of Godliness,* NavPress 2016, Jerry Bridges writes, "The Christian has been delivered from fear of the wrath of God (see 1 John 4:18). But the Christian has not been delivered from the *discipline* of God against his sinful conduct, and in this sense he still fears God. He works out his salvation with fear and trembling (Philippians 2:12); he lives his life as a stranger here in reverent fear (1 Peter 1: 17). For the child of God, however, the primary meaning of the fear of God is veneration and honor, reverence and awe" (page 26).

[50] For more information on love bonds and fear bonds, see *"The Life Model: Living from the Heart Jesus Gave You,"* by James G. Friesen, Ph.D.; E. James Wilder, Ph.D.; Anne M. Bierling, M.A.; Rick Koepcke, M.A.; and Maribeth Poole, M.A., Shepherd's House, Inc., copyright © 2000, pages 16-18.

[51] *"The Life Model: Living from the Heart Jesus Gave You,"* page 17.

[52] ibid, page 16

[53] ibid, page 19

[54] ibid, page 17

[55] Summarized from ibid, pages 18-19.

[56] Panic Attacks and Panic Disorders, HelpGuide.org, http://www.helpguide.org/articles/anxiety/panic-attacks-and-panic-disorders.htm, accessed March 14, 2017.

[57] Activity suggested for panic attacks during a private conversation with Dr. David Wickstrom in July, 2008.

[58] "The Victim Mentality," BecomeSelfAware.com, http://www.becomeselfaware.com/articles/articles-2013/57-the-victim-mentality.html, accessed December 10, 2016.

[59] One list of who we are in Christ, "Bible Verses about Our Identity in Christ," can be accessed at BibleStudyTools.com, http://www.biblestudytools.com/topical-verses/bible-verses-about-our-identity-in-christ/, accessed March 14, 2017.

[60] Key verses include Matthew 18:18-20; Luke 10:19-20; 2 Corinthians 10:3-5; Ephesians 1:19-23; 2:6-7; 3:20; 2 Timothy 1:7 and 2 Peter 1:3.

[61] Examples: Chronicles 20:3-22; Psalms; Ephesians 1:3-12; 3:14-20; Philippians 1:9-11; Colossians 1:9-12.

[62] *The Life Model: Living from the Heart Jesus Gave You*, page 20.

[63] ibid, page 16.

[64] Adapted with permission from *A Theory and Process for Christian Counseling & Inner Healing*, pages 41-43.

[65] "The original Karpman Drama Triangle as it appears in Karpman, S. (1968). Fairy tales and script drama analysis. Transactional Analysis Bulletin, 7(26), 39-43." From https://en.wikipedia.org/wiki/Karpman_drama_triangle, accessed March 14, 2017. For more information on the drama triangle, see https://www.karpmandramatriangle.com/pdf/thenewdramatriangles.pdf, http://therapyideas.net/manipulation.htm, http://www.johngouletmft.com/Breaking_The_Drama_Triangle_Newest.pdf, and https://www.psychologytoday.com/blog/fixing-families/201106/the-relationship-triangle.

[66] Reframe and refocus are concepts from *The Brain That Changes Itself: Stories of Personal Triumph from the Frontiers of Brain Science* by Norman Doidge, M.D, Scribe Publications, Pty Ltd, copyright © 2007.

[67] "Obsessive-Compulsive Disorder: When Unwanted Thoughts or Irresistible Actions Take Over," National Institute of Mental Health, http://www.nimh.nih.gov/health/publications/obsessive-compulsive-disorder-when-unwanted-thoughts-take-over/index.shtml, accessed March 14, 2017.

[68] The word 'control', as often used in this book, refers to unhealthy control.

[69] Healthy control includes directing, regulating, governing, or restraining someone or something that you are in charge of, without attempting to coerce or manipulate them. Healthy control is needed to carry out designated responsibilities well. *For example: training up a child in the way they should go (Proverbs 22:6); driving a car; persevering in a task; exercising self-control.*

[70] Adapted with permission from *A Theory and Process for Christian Counseling & Inner Healing*, pages 10-11.

[71] *Funk & Wagnalls Standard College Dictionary,* copyright © 1977 by Harper & Row, Publishers, Inc.

[72] *Overcoming Addiction: A Common Sense Approach,* by Michael Hardiman, Crossing Press, copyright © 2000, page 13.

[73] Adapted with permission from a talk on *Addictions and Pornography,* presented by Alfred C.W. Davis in Jakarta, November, 2003.

[74] ibid

[75] ibid. Used with permission.

[76] *The Life Model: Living from the Heart Jesus Gave You,* pages 11-12.

[77] "Attachment theory is the joint work of John Bowlby and Mary Ainsworth (Ainsworth & Bowlby, 1991)." Quote from "The Origins of Attachment Theory: John Bowlby and Mary Ainsworth" by Inge Bretherton, Developmental Psychology (1992), 28, 759-775. http://www.psychology.sunysb.edu/attachment/online/inge_origins.pdf, accessed March 21, 2017.

Tim Clinton and Gary Sibcy built on this foundation in *Why You Do the Things You Do: The Secret to Healthy Relationships*, Thomas Nelson, copyright © 2006. Their contribution is the main source of the concepts and descriptions of avoidant, ambivalent and disorganized relationship styles presented in this paragraph.

[78] "The Toyota Production System Works for Relationships, Too" by Ed Batista, Harvard Business Review, April 1, 2016, https://hbr.org/2016/04/the-toyota-production-system-works-for-relationships-too?utm_medium=referral&utm_source=pulsenews, accessed March 14, 2017.

[79] ibid

[80] ibid

[81] ibid

[82] Those still outside Christ have not yet been forgiven or granted the privileges of a believer (Ephesians 2:1-3).

[83] Living in the Path of Peace <http://ent.freemin.org/conflict-management/>

[84] *Counseling Couples in Conflict: A Relational Restoration Model* by Hames N. Sells and Mark A. Yarhouse, ©2011, IVP Academic, location 273-276 Kindle version, concept adapted to a group context.

[85] Concept from *The DNA of Relationships* by Dr. Gary Smalley, ©2004, 2007 Smalley Publishing Group LLC, page 38.

[86] Concept from *Counseling Couples in Conflict: A Relational Restoration Model* by James N. Sells and Mark A. Yarhouse, IVP Academic, copyright © 2011.

[87] In *Secrets of a Prayer Warrior* (Baker Publishing Group, copyright © 2009) Derek Prince lists 12 "instruments" of prayer found in Scripture. These include "praise, thanksgiving, worship, petition, intercession, supplication, command, commitment, dedication, persistence, blessing and cursing" (page 69). See http://prayerstrategists.net/about/resources-by-strategy/ for resources on a variety of extraordinary prayer strategies.

[88] "Our weapons include the name of Jesus, the blood of Christ, the Word of God, fasting, concentrated prayer, agreement in prayer with other believers (on site when possible, but can also be virtual), praise and worship, and persistence." Notes from a March 2013 lunch conversation with J.F.K. Mensah, coauthor of *The Lost Art of Spiritual Warfare*, copyright © 2012 J.F.K. and Georgina Mensah.

[89] "History Belongs to the Intercessors" by Walter Wink, https://celectcdn.s3.amazonaws.com/files/0024/6892/2012.01.08.pastors_blog.pdf, accessed March 16, 2017.

[90] *Not the Way It's Supposed to Be* by Cornelius Plantinga Jr., copyright © 1995 Grand Rapids: William B. Eerdmans Publishing Co., page 10.

[91] "Shalom - Peace be unto you," April 20, 2005, http://peacebeuntoyou.blogspot.co.id/2005/04/shalom-peace-be-unto-you.html, accessed May 27, 2017.

[92] "A Study on Biblical Concepts of Peace in the Old and New Testaments," by Efraim Goldstein, Dec. 1, 1997, December 1997 Jews for Jesus Newsletter (5758:4), http://jewsforjesus.org/publications/newsletter/december-1997/studyonbiblical, accessed May 27, 2017.

Made in the USA
Las Vegas, NV
03 June 2023

72931588R00154